World-Renowned Recipes

Photography
Bernard Enjolras
Translation
id2m

ÉDITIONS OUEST-FRANCE
13, rue du Breil - Rennes

Contents

The History of Mont-Saint-Michel

Mont-Saint-Michel at high tide.
Photo. A. Mauxion

View of the bay from the abbey.

More than a thousand years of history, faith, courage and talent have shaped the "Wonder of the Western World" – this masterpiece and World Heritage Site.

It was in 708 that Archangel Michael appeared to Aubert, Bishop of Avranches, and commanded him to build a chapel at the top of Mont Tombe, a rocky islet in the middle of an immense bay, lashed by the highest tides in Europe.

This marked the beginning of Mont-Saint-Michel and for a thousand years increasingly beautiful and bold additions were made to the structure to form the unique architectural marvel that it is today.

In turn a monastery, Christian spiritual and cultural centre, pilgrimage destination, place of worship, citadel and prison, Mont-Saint-Michel is important in the history of France and Western Christianity.

As a tribute to its glorified past, UNESCO designated Mont-Saint-Michel as a World Heritage Site in 1972.

Evening tide at Mont-Saint-Michel.

The Magic of Mont-Saint-Michel

The Wonder of the Western World, Celestial Jerusalem, Pyramid of the Seas: such were the names given to Mont-Saint-Michel by the pilgrims in the Middle Ages.

Like them, twenty-first century visitors cannot help but be seized by the magic of the place.

Lashed by the highest tides in Europe, the enormous bay stretches for as far as the eye can see, between sea and sky, sand and water, green Normandy and rocky Brittany.

And in the middle, shooting up from the sand stands Mont-Saint-Michel, firmly anchored to its rock. Decorated with stone filigree work, it reaches high into the sky and is crowned with a bronze spire, featuring a statue of Saint Michael bringing down the devil and symbolising the eternal fight between good and evil.

Between the dominating abbey and protective ramparts sits the mediaeval city, with its main street, narrow alleys, gardens and timber-framed houses, which huddle together for protection from the elements.

Far off, the roar of the tide, which rises "as fast as a horse at full gallop", echoes the melodious and enchanting singing of the monks and nuns celebrating their office in the abbey church.

Sometimes, once night has fallen, the whistling wind carries the soft monotonous chant of Tiphaine, wife of Bertrand Du Guesclin, Constable of France, who read the fate of the world in the stars.

The Story of La Mère Poulard

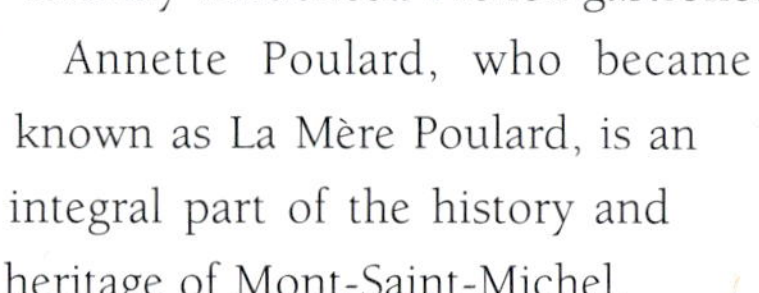

There was once a courageous, talented young woman and cook who profoundly influenced French gastronomy. Annette Poulard, who became known as La Mère Poulard, is an integral part of the history and heritage of Mont-Saint-Michel.

Annette Poulard

Born in 1852, Annette was in her twenties when Mont-Saint-Michel reopened its doors to the world, having been a notorious prison since the French Revolution in 1789.

It was also at this time that young Annette agreed to marry Victor Poulard, son of the Mont-Saint-Michel baker, who remained at her side for the rest of her life. With his support, Annette Poulard devoted her life to her two passions – cooking and Mont-Saint-Michel.

Hospitality is a thousand-year-old tradition on Mont-Saint-Michel. As early as the Middle Ages, the inhabitants of Mont-Saint-Michel – known as the *Montois* – welcomed pilgrims to their inns for food and lodging.

So, in 1888, it seemed natural for Annette and Victor to open their inn to pilgrims and food lovers eager to taste the delights of the woman who was from then on known as La Mère Poulard.

Mont-Saint-Michel's small cemetery bears witness to the beautiful story of Annette and Victor, as visitors can still read the epitaph on the family tomb: "Here lie Annette and Victor Poulard, loving husband and wife, charming hotel-keepers. May God welcome them as they welcomed their guests."

Annette Poulard at 25 years old.

LA NORMANDIE — "La C. P. A.
14. LE MONT SAINT-MICHEL — L'Hôtel de Madame Poulard

When she was not at her stove, La Mère Poulard would welcome guests at the door to her inn.

La Mère Poulard

Annette's immense talent, and the some seven hundred recipes that she developed over her stove, quickly brought her acclaim and earned her the name La Mère Poulard, an honorary title which pays homage to *Mères Cuisinières*, i.e. the most talented women chefs.

Of all her recipes, the omelette went on to become her best-known dish, winning her fame throughout the world.

The causeway that now connects Mont-Saint-Michel to the mainland did not exist in the 1880s and so travellers who arrived on foot, horseback or by carriage had to wait until low tide to cross the bay.

As a result, they arrived at all hours, exhausted by the long, and often testing, journey.

La Mère Poulard kept her large stove permanently lit so her newly arrived guests could warm up and relax, and was able to make her marvellous omelettes within minutes of their arrival.

Instantly won over by La Mère Poulard's cooking, travellers would return home singing her praises.

This marked the start of La Mère Poulard and her omelette's rise to fame.

The famous omelette and delicious biscuits from Mont-Saint-Michel have contributed to the world-renown of La Mère Poulard.

Renown

Today, La Mère Poulard and Mont-Saint-Michel are intrinsically linked.

By the end of the 19th century, the bronze spire, topped with the statue of Saint Michael, had been erected to give Mont-Saint-Michel its current silhouette, and the causeway had been built to connect the island to the mainland.

The small train carrying travellers to the foot of the "Wonder of the Western World" and the advent of the car meant that the site was more accessible and it began to attract crowds of modern-day pilgrims – tourists.

It was at this moment that the Mère Poulard phenomenon really took off, and proof of this can be found in the three thousand five hundred portraits and autographs of celebrities from the world of art, theatre, cinema, sports, economics and politics that adorn the walls of her inn.

La Mère Poulard's omelette – hand-selected eggs, French Normandy butter, a fireplace and some carefully guarded secrets...

Celebrities at La Mère Poulard Restaurant

Although La Mère Poulard never left her stove or Mont-Saint-Michel, she was curious about the world, and travelled in her own way, by welcoming guests from every horizon.

She liked to remember people through messages left in the visitors' book, signed photographs and sketches drawn as meals were coming to a close.

La Mère Poulard Inn has continued the tradition, and today you can take a journey back through history, thanks to all the paintings, drawings and photographs on display.

You'll soon discover that King Edward VII and the British Royal Family, who were regular guests of La Mère Poulard's at the turn of the last century, contributed a great deal to her fame.

United States President Theodore Roosevelt and French Prime Minister Georges Clemenceau – First World War hero, friend of La Mère Poulard and admirer of her cooking – also contributed to her growing world-renown.

They would of course have been astonished to learn that in 1923, the young Chou En-lai stayed at La Mère Poulard Inn before returning to China where, twenty-five years later, he took part in the Chinese Revolution alongside fellow traveller Mao Tse-tung.

De gauche à droite : Patton, Bradley et Montgomery.

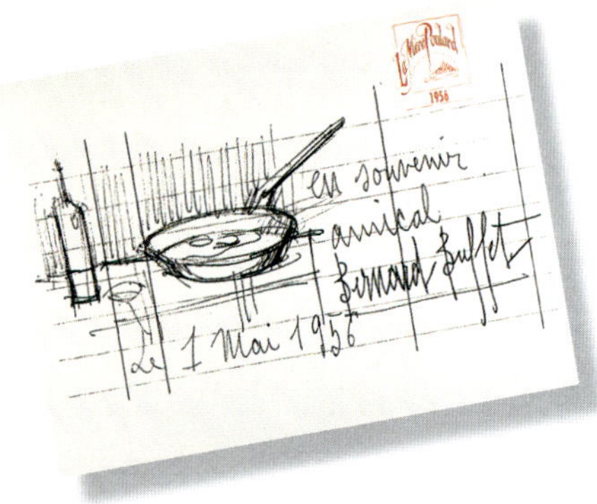

Had he visited a few years later, the future Chinese Prime Minister could have met another revolutionary – the deposed Trotsky, who was beginning his exile in style. Here, Trotsky could mingle with the great names in finance and industry – the Rothschilds and Rockefellers – who were regular customers of La Mère Poulard throughout the twentieth century.

Of all the royal visitors to her inn, La Mère Poulard was particularly fond of Prince and Princess Takamatsu of the Japanese Imperial family, and the numerous exiled Russian princes and princesses, who regularly visited the inn to socialise and drown their sorrows until the early hours of the morning.

No doubt La Mère Poulard would have been delighted to see that on the hundredth anniversary of her inn, the *Entente Cordiale* was being celebrated by British Prime Minister Margaret Thatcher and French President François Mitterrand, who had come to discuss world affairs over a good meal.

She would also have been proud to learn that her inn served as a headquarters for the Normandy landings in 1944, and that during these difficult times, as in the years of commemoration that followed, General Patton, General Bradley and Marshal Montgomery enjoyed her dishes much in the same way as Winston Churchill, the famous statesman and renowned epicurean, did.

Ernest Hemingway spent several days at a table in La Mère Poulard Inn writing about the main events of the Normandy landings.

As a connoisseur, he must have noticed the comments made by French singer Maurice Chevalier a few years earlier, describing his stay at the inn as, "A splendid place – Good food – Good service – Delightful owners – I'll come again!"

Such names are not surprising given that Mont-Saint-Michel and La Mère Poulard attracted all kinds of artists, like the painter Foujita, who drew a small cat, Bernard Buffet, who drew a frying pan, and more surprisingly, the American actor Charlton Heston, who sketched Mont-Saint-Michel with talent and extraordinary speed.

So many artists fell in love with La Mère Poulard Inn and a few are cited below as if in a poem by the French poet Prévert – Claude Monet, Jean Cocteau, Marcel Pagnol, André Malraux, Françoise Sagan, Jean Gabin, Rita Hayworth, Jean-Paul Belmondo, Woody Allen, Glenn Glose, Juliette Binoche, Arthur Rubinstein, Jean-Michel Jarre, Charles Aznavour, Christian Dior and Yves Saint Laurent.

Finally, we must not forget the outstanding men who would have been adored by La Mère Poulard. Charles Lindbergh visited after crossing the Atlantic and Alan Shepard went into space before returning to La Mère Poulard Restaurant.

And we shall of course leave the conclusion to the King of French cuisine, Paul Bocuse, for whom "La Mère Poulard is France."

Ernest Hemingway at La Mère Poulard Restaurant during the Normandy landings in 1944.

Returning from a day of fishing scallops.

Treasures of the Bay

Beyond its magical atmosphere and spectacular tides, the Bay of Mont-Saint-Michel is dotted with treasures between the land and sea, the salt meadows and polders and between Normandy and Brittany.

The sea

It is the English Channel that rushes into the Bay of Mont-Saint-Michel and washes onto its shores. From Granville, in Normandy, to Cancale, in Brittany, the Bay of Mont-Saint-Michel is bursting with fish and shellfish.

On the Normandy side, you can find scallops and whelks from Granville harbour, and large Chausey Island lobsters, whose fishing is strictly controlled and permitted to a few local fishermen only.

On the other side of the bay, the Breton harbour of Cancale is renowned for oyster farming, while a large part of the coastline is lined with wooden stakes, so typical of mussel farming in the area.

The last fishermen to fish on foot in the bay collect shellfish and hunt for shrimps using heavy nets, which they tirelessly push out in front of them.

Further out to sea, flotillas of small fishing boats catch sea bass, mackerel, sole, plaice and turbot, and pull up pots filled with crabs and spider crabs from the seabed.

Finally, some of the more experienced anglers fish the salmon which swim up the rivers Sée and Sélune. This species was once so abundant that local farmers and labourers working on Mont-Saint-Michel specified in their contracts that they were not to be fed salmon more than three times a week!

Oyster beds in the bay.

Mont-Saint-Michel's salt-meadow sheep.

The salt meadows

The salt meadows are typical of the Bay of Mont-Saint-Michel and the vegetation that grows on the shore there is regularly covered by the sea when the tide comes in.

It is here that salt-meadow sheep are raised, a tradition that dates back to the Middle Ages.

The sheep spend much of their lives grazing in the salt meadows, and their meat consequently has an unparalleled flavour.

During the Easter festivities, the first lambs of the season are ready to be eaten, and thus contribute, albeit involuntarily, to the renown of Bay of Mont-Saint-Michel gastronomy.

A salt-meadow lamb.

The polders

The polders form another distinctive landscape in the bay.

It was in the 19th century that the polders – areas stolen from the sea by the construction of protective dams – took shape in the Bay of Mont-Saint-Michel.

This extremely fertile land is particularly used to grow vegetables; for example sweet carrots, new potatoes, crunchy lettuce and even pink shallots, a variety specific to the bay.

Lettuce and carrots from the polders of Mont-Saint-Michel.

Collecting cider apples.

The area around the bay

Further inland, the polders give way to Normandy and Brittany's farms. It is here that you'll find corn-fed chickens, duck raised for their *foie gras,* farmhouse pigs, Normandy and Breton cows, eggs, milk, butter and cream.

The countryside is also dotted with apple and pear orchards, cider and perry producers and you can sometimes even find farmhouse *Calvados,* or apple-brandy, made just like in the good old days, when the still went from farm to farm, distilling the precious few litres of alcohol that kept the farmers warm throughout the long winter.

Spring Recipes

In springtime, the lambs go out into the bay's salt meadows and graze blissfully on the soft grass. But this is just a fleeting moment of happiness, as the spit is already turning ready for the traditional Easter roast.

Spring Starters

Crunchy spring vegetable soup

Serves 6 to 8

Preparation: 30 to 40 minutes
Cooking time: 1 hour

100 G (3.5 OZ) RIPE TOMATOES
100 G (3.5 OZ) BABY CARROTS
1 SMALL COURGETTE
1 ONION
1 SHALLOT
1 STALK OF CELERY
2 SMALL TURNIPS
2 GARLIC CLOVES
50 G (2 OZ) GREEN BEANS, TOPPED AND TAILED
50 G (2 OZ) PEAS, SHELLED
50 G (2 OZ) BUTTER
1.5 LITRES (2 1/2 PINTS) MINERAL WATER (PREFERABLY *PLANCOËT*)
50 G (2 OZ) FRESH HERBS, CHOPPED AND MIXED
1 DOZEN CROUTONS, GRILLED
8 THIN SLICES OF BACON

Clean, peel and wash all the vegetables.
Cut the tomatoes, carrots and courgette into cubes, then chop the onion, shallot and garlic. Cut the celery and green beans into small strips, slice the turnips and leave the peas whole.
Fry all the vegetables in 50 g (2 oz) of butter and then add the herbs.
Cover the vegetables with 1.5 litres (2 1/2 pints) of *Plancoët* mineral water and leave to cook on a low heat for 1 hour.
During this time, regularly skim off the foam.
Then, halfway through cooking (i.e. after about 30 minutes) add the eight thin slices of bacon.
Once the hour is up and the soup is cooked, cover the pan with a tea towel. Pop the lid on the pan to preserve all the flavour and leave it to stew for 2 to 3 hours.
Reheat this crunchy soup and serve with small grilled croutons.

Velvety watercress soup with swirls of cream

Serves 4

Preparation: 15 minutes
Cooking time: 30 minutes

500 G (1.1 LB) POTATOES
1 BUNCH OF WATERCRESS
1.5 LITRES (2 1/2 PINTS) MINERAL WATER
40 G (1.5 OZ) BUTTER
200 ML (7 FL OZ) THICK DOUBLE CREAM
FRESHLY GROUND SALT AND PEPPER
A FEW OVEN TOASTED CROUTONS

Wash the watercress thoroughly, then peel and wash the potatoes and cut them into quarters.
Melt the butter in a pan and then add the roughly chopped watercress.
Sauté for 1 to 2 minutes. Then add the mineral water and the potatoes with some salt and leave to cook for 30 minutes.
During this time, lightly whisk the 200 ml (7 fl oz) of cream in a pre-chilled mixing bowl, adding salt and pepper as you go. Whisk the cream delicately until it looks almost like whipped cream.
Once the soup is cooked, transfer to a blender or food processor and blend until smooth.
Season to taste.
Then pour into soup dishes, add some toasted croutons and then a dollop of seasoned whipped cream.

Velvety watercress soup with swirls of cream

Mont-Saint-Michel style stuffed clams

Serves 4

Preparation: 15 minutes
Cooking time: 5 min. for the clams, 10 minutes under the grill

800 G (1.8 LB) CLAMS
180 G (6.3 OZ) SALTED BUTTER
3 SHALLOTS, FINELY CHOPPED
3 GARLIC CLOVES, DEGERMED AND FINELY CHOPPED
1/2 BUNCH OF PARSLEY, CHOPPED
1/2 BUNCH OF CHIVES, CHOPPED
FRESHLY GROUND SALT AND PEPPER
1 SPOONFUL OF *CALVADOS*
2 SPOONFULS OF CROUTONS, DRY AND ROUGHLY CHOPPED
2 SPOONFULS OF BREADCRUMBS

Open the clams naturally in a little water.
Remove the meat and keep the bottom half of the shell.
Arrange the shells side by side in an oven-proof dish.
Now, prepare the clam stuffing. Mix the soft butter with the shallots, garlic and herbs, a little salt (the butter is already salted), pepper, a spoonful of *Calvados* and a spoonful of roughly chopped croutons.
Stuff each clam with this mixture.
Lightly sprinkle each one with the breadcrumb mixture.
Pre-heat the grill to 180-200°C (350-400°F/Gas mark 5) and pop them under it for 10 minutes.

Mont-Saint-Michel style stuffed clams.

Savoury leek pie

Serves 4

Preparation: 30 minutes
Cooking time: 30 + 30 minutes at 180°C (350°F/Gas mark 4)

400 G (14 OZ) PUFF PASTRY
400 G (14 OZ) YOUNG LEEKS
100 G (3.5 OZ) FRESH FARMHOUSE BACON
160 G (5.6 OZ) SINGLE CREAM
50 G (2 OZ) + 30 G (1 OZ) UNSALTED BUTTER
50 G (2 OZ) FLOUR
50 G (2 OZ) BUTTON MUSHROOMS, SLICED
1 GRATED NUTMEG
3 SPOONFULS OF HERBS (PARSLEY, CHERVIL, CHIVES, CORIANDER), CHOPPED
1 EGG YOLK FOR GLAZING
FRESHLY GROUND SALT AND PEPPER

Trim the leeks, then wash and slice them finely.
Cut the bacon into cubes and chop all of the fresh herbs.
Make a bechamel sauce as follows: melt 50 g (2 oz) of butter, then add 50 g (2 oz) of flour and cook for 5 minutes on low heat, stirring constantly. Bring the single cream to the boil and gradually pour into the mixture. Season with salt, pepper and nutmeg, and cook for about 5 minutes, until thickened.
Once the sauce has been made, melt 30 g (1 oz) of butter in a pan, and then add the bacon, the leeks and the sliced button mushrooms.
Cook for about 10 to 15 minutes.
Next, add the chopped herbs and the bechamel sauce.
Boil for 5 minutes and leave to cool.
While the mixture is cooling, roll out the puff pastry and make two circles of about 26 to 30 centimetres (10-12 ").
Use one of the circles to line a chilled, deep tin and then pour the filling onto the pastry.
Use the second circle to cover the pie, folding the outside edges back in towards the centre.
Brush the pastry with a glaze (an egg yolk thinned with a little water, some salt and pepper). Then make a hole in the centre (to let out the steam) and cook at 180°C (350°F/Gas mark 4) for 30 minutes.

Eggs *en cocotte* with spinach from the bay

Serves 4

Preparation: 10 to 15 minutes
Cooking time (bain marie): 15 to 20 minutes at 180°C (350°F/Gas mark 4)

200 G (7 OZ) BABY SPINACH LEAVES
4 LARGE SLICES OF DRY CURED HAM
4 LARGE EGGS
4 SPOONFULS OF *CRÈME FRAÎCHE*
1 SPOONFUL OF CURLY LEAF PARSLEY, FINELY CHOPPED
20 G (0.7 OZ) BUTTER
FRESHLY GROUND SALT AND PEPPER

Thoroughly wash the baby spinach leaves and remove the stems. Pat them dry and then sweat in butter for a few minutes.
Line individual dishes or ramekins with slices of drycured ham.
Place half the spinach in the bottom of the dishes, then crack an egg into each one. Top with a few baby spinach leaves, a dollop of *crème fraîche,* and a little finely chopped curly leaf parsley.
Add salt and pepper.
Cook for 15 to 20 minutes in a bain marie at 180°C (350°F/Gas mark 4), according to how you like them.
Serve with a slice of toasted farmhouse bread.

Breton artichoke and shrimp salad

Serves 4

Preparation: about 30 minutes

4 LARGE BRETON ARTICHOKES, PRE-BOILED
500 G (1.1 LB) SHRIMPS, PRE-COOKED
SEVERAL SPRIGS OF CHERVIL
400 ML (13.5 FL OZ) VINAIGRETTE, MADE FROM WINE VINEGAR, NUT OIL, SALT, PEPPER AND 1 TSP MUSTARD

Peel away the artichoke's large outer leaves and put them to one side.
Remove the artichoke's choke and heart, wash them and then chop them finely.
Fill each large artichoke leaf with the chopped artichoke mixture.
Peel the shrimps and arrange on each artichoke leaf.
Drizzle with vinaigrette, garnish with sprigs of chervil and serve.

Little *chouquettes* with samphire from the bay

Serves 6 to 8

Preparation: 25 to 30 minutes
Cooking time: 30 to 35 minutes, preheat oven to 180-190°C (350-375°F/Gas mark 4-5)

250 ML (9 FL OZ) WATER
100 G (3.5 OZ) BUTTER
100 G (3.5 OZ) FLOUR
4 EGGS
60 G (2 OZ) GRATED GRUYÈRE CHEESE
40 G (1.5 OZ) CAMEMBERT, CUT INTO CUBES
40 G (1.5 OZ) SAMPHIRE, COOKED AND CUT INTO SMALL PIECES
FRESHLY GROUND SALT AND PEPPER

Put the water, butter, salt and pepper into a pan and bring to the boil.
When the butter has melted, take the pan off the heat and add the sifted flour in one go.
Stir vigorously with a spatula or wooden spoon until the mixture is smooth and forms a ball.
Put the pan back on the heat and continue stirring until the mixture dries out, i.e. it no longer sticks to the pan or spatula.
Take the pan back off the heat and add the eggs to the mixture one by one.
Mix well and cool the mixture slightly by stirring it constantly. Now add the samphire, Gruyère and Camembert.
Form little balls using a spoon and arrange them on a baking sheet. Season each one with freshly ground pepper and pop in the oven to cook for about 30 minutes.
Serve as appetisers or with a small dandelion leaf salad.

Breton artichoke and shrimp salad

Duo of salmon in a fresh herb marinade

Duo of salmon in a fresh herb marinade

Serves 4

Preparation: 25 to 30 minutes
To be made 10 hours in advance

200 G (10.5 OZ) FRESH SALMON FILLETS
200 G (10.5 OZ) FRESH SMOKED SALMON
100 G (3.5 OZ) SMALL SHRIMPS, PEELED
1 LEMON
1 OR 2 SHALLOTS
1 GENEROUS HANDFUL OF FRESH THYME
2 TBSP FINELY CHOPPED FENNEL AND DILL
100 ML (3.5 FL OZ) OLIVE OIL
FRESH HERBS
FRESHLY GROUND SALT AND PEPPER

If not already done, slice the smoked salmon and cut the fresh salmon into thin slices.
Squeeze lemon juice onto the shrimps, add salt and pepper and leave them to marinate for a few minutes.
Peel and finely chop the shallots and add the thyme, fresh herbs, fennel and dill. Add this mixture to the marinating shrimps.
Pour the marinade over the duo of salmon, drizzle with olive oil and leave to marinate for 10 hours. Turn over the pieces of salmon two or three times during this time.
Serve this marinade on a large plate with a fresh herb salad.

Spring pea and *confit* duck gizzard salad

Serves 4

Preparation: 25 minutes

A FEW LEAVES OF EARLY OR SPRING LETTUCE
200 G (7 OZ) CONFIT DUCK GIZZARDS
20 G (0.7 OZ) GRILLED HAZELNUTS
100 G (3.5 OZ) FRESH PEAS, SHELLED AND COOKED
100 ML (3.5 FL OZ) SINGLE CREAM
200 ML (7 FL OZ) VINAIGRETTE MADE FROM XERES VINEGAR, GRAPESEED OIL, SALT AND PEPPER
1 BUNCH OF PARSLEY
FRESHLY GROUND SALT AND PEPPER

Thoroughly wash the lettuce leaves and then store them in the fridge.
Thinly slice the confit duck gizzards.
Roughly chop the grilled hazelnuts.
Blend half of the peas. Add the 100 ml (3.5 fl oz) of single cream, blend again and season. Then sieve the mixture to remove any bits of pea shell.
Make 200 ml (7 fl oz) of vinaigrette with the Xeres vinegar, grapeseed oil, salt and pepper.
Heat the gizzards and vinaigrette in a pan so they are just warm (do not allow to boil).
Using a spoon, spread the cream of peas on the bottom of four white porcelain plates.
Arrange the lettuce leaves and warm gizzards in the centre of the plates. Top with the remaining cold peas and grilled hazelnuts.
Drizzle with the vinaigrette used to warm the gizzards.
Garnish with parsley if desired.

Spring Main Courses

Serves 4

Preparation: 30 minutes
Cooking time: 10 min

8 TO 12 ABALONES, DEPENDING ON THEIR SIZE
1 TSP OLIVE OIL
100 G (3.5 OZ) UNSALTED BUTTER
2 SHALLOTS, CHOPPED
1 BUNCH OF FLAT LEAF PARSLEY
CHOPPED PARSLEY
250 G (9 OZ) MUSHROOMS, HORN-OF-PLENTY

Fried abalone with horn-of-plenty mushrooms

Shell the abalones, trim the head, gills and viscera, and wash thoroughly in cold water. Cut each one into three slices, then lengthwise into smaller strips.
Pour the oil and butter into a non-stick frying pan.
Lightly fry the shallots and add the abalone strips. Add pepper (but not salt).
Cook for about 5 minutes, and no longer.
Then add the chopped parsley.
Remove the abalone from the butter and replace with the washed and dried mushrooms.
Cook for 5 minutes then remove from the pan.
Arrange a few mushrooms in the bottom of each washed abalone shell.
Top with the abalone strips, drizzle with the cooking butter and heat in the oven for a few minutes.
Garnish with sprigs of parsley and serve.

Serves 4

Preparation: about 20 minutes
Cooking time: 20 minutes

4 TROUT, EACH WEIGHING 250 G (9 OZ)
80 G (3 OZ) GOURMET *FLEUR DE SEL* SEA SALT
4 TSP OLIVE OIL
4 SPRIGS OF FLOWERING THYME, FLOWERING WILD THYME, FLOWERING SAVORY
4 SLICES OF LEMON
1 PINCH OF CRUSHED PEPPERCORNS
12 SMALL POTATOES, COOKED IN THEIR SKINS

Grilled trout with sea salt and wild herbs

Remove the thyme, wild thyme and savory flowers from their stems and then mix with the salt and pepper.
Sprinkle this mixture all over the gutted, washed and dried fish.
Position the trout on a grill or barbecue, drizzle with olive oil and grill for 10 minutes on each side.
Once cooked, garnish with a slice of lemon and serve hot with a few potatoes.

Fried abalone with horn-of-plenty mushrooms

Fillet of brill with caramelised onions

Serves 4

Preparation: 25 minutes
Cooking time: 30 min. for the onions, 5 minutes for the brill

8 SPRING ONIONS OR
200 G (7 OZ) SMALL ONIONS
50 G (2 OZ) BUTTER
250 ML (9 FL OZ) MUSCADET
1 PINCH OF SUGAR
4 LARGE BRILL FILLETS, WEIGHING FROM 150-180 G (5-6.3 OZ)
FRESHLY GROUND SALT AND PEPPER

Melt the butter.
Lightly sweat the 8 spring onions, cut in two lengthwise, or the 200 g (7 oz) of peeled small onions.
Add salt, pepper and a pinch of sugar.
Once the onions have caramelised, pour in the Muscadet.
Bring to the boil and add the seasoned brill fillets.
Cook for 5 minutes, depending on the thickness of the fillets.
Serve hot.

Fillet of brill with caramelised onions

Pork tenderloin with spring turnips

Pork tenderloin with spring turnips

Do not peel the turnips, but scrape the skin off, being careful not to remove the tops.
Melt the butter in a frying pan and then brown the turnips.
Add the pork tenderloin and season.
Cook for a few minutes and then add the water and a pinch of sugar.
Check the seasoning.
Continue cooking for about 15 minutes, basting often.
Once the tenderloin is cooked, cut into slices.
Serve on warm plates.
Surround the tenderloin slices with the turnips and pour on the gravy.

Serves 4

Preparation: 20 minutes
Cooking time: 30 minutes

600 G (1.3 LB) PORK TENDERLOIN
800 G (1.8 LB) SMALL SPRING TURNIPS
50 G (2 OZ) BUTTER
200 ML (7 FL OZ) WATER (APPROXIMATELY)
1 TSP SUGAR
FRESHLY GROUND SALT AND PEPPER

Spring lamb sauté
with early vegetables

Spring lamb *sauté* with early vegetables

Serves 4 to 8

Preparation: 1 hour
Cooking time: 1 1/2 hours

600 G (1.3 LB) LAMB SHOULDER, CUT INTO PIECES
600 G (1.3 LB) LAMB NECK, CUT INTO PIECES
400 G (14 OZ) LAMB BREAST, CUT INTO PIECES
1 BOUQUET GARNI
400 G (14 OZ) TOMATOES
2 GARLIC CLOVES
200 G (7 OZ) TURNIPS, PEELED
200 G (7 OZ) SPRING CARROTS, PEELED
200 G (7 OZ) PEAS, SHELLED
200 G (7 OZ) MANGETOUT
200 G (7 OZ) GREEN BEANS
2 SPOONFULS OF OLIVE OIL
4 SHALLOTS
4 SPRING ONIONS
FRESHLY GROUND SALT AND PEPPER

Put the pieces of lamb in a casserole and brown in a little olive oil.
Once browned, remove the lamb from the casserole and then add the shallots and spring onions, peeled and cut into two.
Next, add the tomatoes, cut into cubes, and the carrots and turnips.
Put the pieces of lamb on top.
Add the bouquet garni and chopped garlic, and cover with cold water.
Season.
Bring to the boil and cook, remembering to skim off the foam regularly.
During this time, shell the peas and prepare the mangetout and green beans.
Lightly cook these vegetables separately. Drain and refresh in cold water.
After 1 1/2 hours, transfer the cooked *sauté* to warm plates.
Reheat the peas, mangetout and beans in a little knob of butter.
Sprinkle the vegetables over the lamb *sauté* and serve hot.

Locally caught turbot with duo of parsley

Melt the butter in a casserole.
Lightly fry the pieces of turbot in the butter.
Add the two bunches of parsley.
Season lightly. Add the Muscadet and simmer for 15 to 20 minutes, being careful not to let the fish dry out.
Once the fish is cooked, remove from the casserole and reduce the gravy until it resembles a sugary green syrup.
Filter the sauce.
Reheat the turbot.
Garnish with a few parsley leaves and serve with the gravy, in a small dish, and a few pieces of leek cooked in butter.

Serves 4

Preparation: 30 minutes
Cooking time: 30 minutes

4 LARGE PIECES OF TURBOT
1 LARGE BUNCH OF FLAT-LEAF PARSLEY, WASHED + A FEW LEAVES
1 LARGE BUNCH OF CURLY-LEAF PARSLEY, WASHED + A FEW LEAVES
4 OR 5 SPOONFULS OF BUTTER
500 ML (17 FL OZ) MUSCADET
1 PINCH OF FRESHLY GROUND SALT AND PEPPER

Garniture
4 LARGE LEEKS, BOILED
20 G (0.7 OZ) BUTTER

Locally caught turbot with duo of parsley

Roast veal with smoky herb gravy

Serves 4

Preparation: 30 minutes
Cooking time: 1 1/4 hours in total

1 RACK OF VEAL OR
600 G TO 800 G (1.3-1.8 LB) ROASTING VEAL
4 SLICES OF FARMHOUSE BACON
4 SHALLOTS
4 CLOVES OF GARLIC
12 ROSEVAL POTATOES
1 SPRIG OF ROSEMARY
1 SPRIG OF THYME
3 BAY LEAVES
1 GLASS OF CIDER
10 G (0.35 OZ) BUTTER
1 TBSP PEANUT OIL
FRESHLY GROUND SALT AND PEPPER

Heat the butter and oil in a casserole. Season the veal with salt and pepper and brown on all sides.
Add the shallots, garlic cloves, bay leaves, sprigs of rosemary and thyme, and leave to simmer for a few minutes.
Next, add the cider and slices of farmhouse bacon. Cover and cook for about 45 minutes.
Once the time is up, add the washed – but not peeled – potatoes to the roast. Cover again and leave to cook for a further 15 minutes.
After this time, remove the veal but leave the potatoes and bacon to cook for another 10 minutes, basting them with the gravy.
Once the potatoes are cooked, cut the rack of veal into four slices and serve with the shallots, garlic cloves, gravy and potatoes.

Roast leg of salt-meadow lamb *en croûte*

Serves 8 to 10

Preparation: 40 minutes
Cooking time: 1 to 1 1/4 hours, depending on the size of the joint

1 LEG OF SALT-MEADOW LAMB
1 SPRIG OF THYME
800 G TO 1 KG (1.8-2.2 LB) PUFF PASTRY
A FEW CRUSHED COFFEE BEANS
1 EGG YOLK MIXED WITH
A LITTLE WATER

For the gravy:

300 TO 500 G (10.5 OZ-1.1 LB) LAMB BONE,
BROKEN INTO PIECES
CRUSHED COFFEE BEANS
2 SHALLOTS
1 CARROT
1 LARGE ONION
1 BUNCH OF FRESH THYME
2 TOMATOES
1 GLASS OF WHITE WINE
1 PINCH OF FRESHLY GROUND SALT AND PEPPER

A few hours before cooking, take the leg of lamb out of the fridge and rub it with the thyme, salt and crushed coffee beans.
Roll out the puff pastry and then wrap the lamb in it to form a parcel.
Glaze the pastry (with the egg yolk and water) and then season with salt and pepper.
Pop the joint on a roasting dish and then put it in the fridge.
Meanwhile, make the gravy with the onion, carrot, shallots, thyme, crushed coffee beans, white wine, tomatoes and a few lamb bones (available from the butcher).
Preheat the oven to 180°C (350°F/Gas mark 4) and cook for about 1 hour. When the crust turns a nice golden colour, reduce the oven temperature to 160°C (325°F/Gas mark 3) to finish cooking the meat.
To check the meat is cooked, insert a skewer into the centre and then bring it to your lip (careful not to burn yourself!). If the tip is hot to the touch, the meat will be cooked to medium; if it's warm, the meat will be rare. Both are perfect ways to enjoy a leg of lamb.
Remove the meat from the oven and leave to rest for about 30 minutes. Then cut the lamb into generous slices and sprinkle each one with a little salt and crushed coffee bean.
Serve with fresh green beans or butter beans and the lamb gravy.

Roast veal with smoky herb gravy

Spring Desserts

Serves 4

Preparation: A few minutes
Reheating in the oven: 20 to 30 minutes at 80°C 180°F/Gas mark 1/4)

1 CAMEMBERT
100 G (2 OZ) MIXED HERBS (DILL, CHERVIL, PARSLEY, CORIANDER, ETC.)
1 TSP GROUND SPICES (PEPPER, CORIANDER, SZECHUAN PEPPER, PINK PEPPERCORNS, CARDAMOM, MACE)
1 TSP DOUBLE CREAM
VINAIGRETTE MADE FROM CIDER VINEGAR AND OLIVE OIL

Baked Camembert with garden herbs and spices

Remove the lid from the Camembert box.
Partly unwrap the cheese and then return it to its box so that the paper falls over the edges.
Top the Camembert with the mixed spices and double cream.
Pop the Camembert in the oven at 80-100°C (180-210°F/Gas mark 1/4) for approximately 20 to 30 minutes.
The Camembert is ready once it becomes soft and runny in the middle.
Put the cheese on a plate and serve it with the mixed herb salad and the cider and olive oil vinaigrette.
Give each guest a spoon so that they can spread the hot Camembert on slices of farmhouse bread.

Serves 6 to 8

Preparation: 30 minutes
Cooking time: a few minutes in a deep fat fryer (160°C/325°F/Gas mark 3)

400 G (14 OZ) SIFTED FLOUR
150 G (5 OZ) GRANULATED SUGAR
70 G (2.5 OZ) CASTER SUGAR
250 ML (9 FL OZ) WATER
5 EGGS
140 G (4.8 OZ) BUTTER
PINCH OF SALT
80 G (2.8 OZ) COOKING CHOCOLATE IN CHIPS OR CHUNKS

Chocolate chip fritters

Mix the butter, water, caster sugar and salt in a pan and bring to the boil.
Once boiling, remove from heat and add the sifted flour in one go, stirring with a wooden spoon.
Reheat gently, letting the mixture dry out for a few minutes.
Remove from heat and add the eggs, one by one.
Let the mixture cool down and then carefully add the chocolate chips.
Using two spoons, drop small round spoonfuls of the mixture into a hot deep fat fryer.
The fritters will turn themselves over once they are nice and golden on one side.
When the fritters are cooked, remove them from the oil, place them on kitchen paper and then sprinkle them with the granulated sugar.
Leave to cool for a few minutes.
Serve warm on the outside and very hot on the inside.
The chocolate will melt in your mouth!

Baked Camembert with garden herbs and spices

Serves 4 to 8

Preparation: 25 to 30 minutes

600 G (1.3 LB) LARGE STRAWBERRIES (PREFERABLY FROM PLOUGASTEL)
200 G (7 OZ) CASTER SUGAR
500 ML (17 FL OZ) EARLY CIDER
12 LEMON GRASS LEAVES
4 SCOOPS OF VANILLA ICE CREAM
200 ML (7 FL OZ) CREAM WHIPPED WITH
40 G (1.5 OZ) ICING SUGAR

Spring strawberry rosette in sweet cider sauce

Hull the strawberries and cut into even slices.
Arrange a layer of strawberry slices in four 8 to 10 cm (3-4") round rings, with at least three lemon grass leaves in the centre of each one.
Top each with more strawberry slices and then arrange in a deep square dish.
Meanwhile, heat the cider with the 200 g (7 oz) of sugar.
Boil until reduced by half.
Let the cider cool a little and then pour over the strawberries.
Refrigerate overnight.
The next day, arrange the rings of strawberry slices in bowls and pour some cider sauce over each one.
Just before serving, remove the rings, add a dollop of whipped cream to the middle of the strawberries and a generous scoop of vanilla ice cream.
Serve cold with the cider sauce.

Spring strawberry rosette in sweet cider sauce

Chocolate and coffee cream dessert

Chocolate and coffee cream dessert

Serves 4

Preparation: 20 to 30 minutes
To be prepared the night before

200 G (7 OZ) QUALITY PLAIN CHOCOLATE
1 TSP COFFEE ESSENCE
80 G (2.8 OZ) UNSALTED BUTTER
250 ML (9 FL OZ) SINGLE CREAM
160 G (5.6 OZ) SUGAR
4 LARGE EGGS
1 SPOONFUL OF *CALVADOS*

Crack open the eggs, separating the whites and yolks into two different bowls. Add the sugar to the yolks and beat well until light and fluffy.
Break the chocolate into small pieces then melt it, along with the cream and butter, in a bain marie. Once melted, add the coffee essence and *Calvados*.
Pour this mixture onto the egg yolks and mix well until the mixture becomes warm. Then whisk the egg whites until stiff.
Fold the whites and yolks together until you have a mousse-like mixture.
Then pour this mixture into small ramekins, glasses or pots.
Chill in the fridge for 5 or 6 hours or prepare the day before and chill overnight. You can use more or less chocolate or coffee according to your personal taste. In this case, the creams will either have a stronger coffee or chocolate flavour.

Honey Madeleines

Spring strawberry roulade

Serves 6 to 8

Preparation: 40 minutes
Cooking time: 15 to 20 minutes

125 G (4.5 OZ) FLOUR
125 G (4.5 OZ) CASTER SUGAR
4 EGGS
1 SACHET OF VANILLA SUGAR
1 SACHET OF BAKING POWDER
20 G (0.7 OZ) SALTED BUTTER
1 JAR OF STRAWBERRY JAM
A LITTLE ICING SUGAR

Beat the egg yolks and sugar in a large stainless steel bowl until light and fluffy.
Gently fold in the sifted flour, vanilla sugar and baking powder.
Then fold in the whipped egg whites.
The mixture should not be too runny.
Pour the mixture into a 5 cm (2") deep, greased, floured or lined square tin.
Bake at 200°C (400°F/Gas mark 6) for about 15 minutes.
Turn the roulade out of its tin and leave to cool.
When cool, spread the jam over the roulade and roll it up, using cling film or a damp tea towel.
When cold, cut the roulade into slices and dust with icing sugar.

Honey Madeleines

Serves 4

Preparation: 20 to 25 minutes
Cooking time: 15 minutes

150 G (5 OZ) CASTER SUGAR
20 G (0.7 OZ) COARSE SUGAR
1 TBSP HONEY
1/2 SACHET OF YEAST
140 G (4.9 OZ) FLOUR
130 G (4.5 OZ) UNSALTED BUTTER
5 EGGS

Crack open the eggs, separating the whites and yolks.
Whisk the egg yolks and caster sugar together in a bowl and then add the softened butter and honey.
Whisk again until the mixture becomes pale.
Meanwhile, preheat the oven to 150-180°C (300-350°F/Gas mark 2-4).
Whisk the egg whites until stiff.
Mix the yeast and flour together.
Then gradually add the egg white and the flour, a spoonful at a time, to the sugar, egg yolk and butter mixture. Fold the mixture until all the ingredients are evenly incorporated.
Grease the Madeleines tin and then pour in the mixture so that the holes are two-thirds full. Sprinkle with coarse sugar and bake for about 15 minutes, depending on the size of the Madeleines.
When cooked, ease the Madeleines out of the tin and leave to cool. When cold, store in an air-tight container.

Caramel-topped poached meringue

Serves 8

Preparation: 35 minutes
Cooking time: 15 minutes

80 ML (3.2 FL OZ) MILK
1 VANILLA POD
6 EGGS
PINCH OF SALT
40 G (1.5 OZ) CASTER SUGAR
120 G (4.2 OZ) CARAMEL
1 LITRE (1 3/4 PINTS) VANILLA FLAVOURED CUSTARD

Split and scrape out the vanilla pod and then boil it with the milk.
Separate the egg whites from the yolks.
Whisk the egg whites with the caster sugar and a pinch of salt until very stiff.
Spoon dollops of the egg white into the simmering milk.
Cook for 2 to 3 minutes, remembering to turn them over, and then drain on kitchen paper.
Then drizzle the liquid caramel over the egg whites to create a dessert that is soft on the inside and crunchy on the outside.
Serve with a vanilla flavoured custard.

Golden raisin semolina cake

Serves 6

Preparation: 30 minutes
Cooking time: 35 minutes

100 G (3.5 OZ) FINE SEMOLINA
500 ML (17 FL OZ) MILK
500 ML (17 FL OZ) SINGLE CREAM
1 VANILLA POD
100 G (3.5 OZ) CASTER SUGAR
50 G (2 OZ) CANE SUGAR
150 G (5 OZ) RAISINS, GOLDEN OR DARK
2 EGGS
2 EGG YOLKS
40 ML (1.5 FL OZ) *CALVADOS*
3 TBSP WATER

Soak the raisins in the *Calvados*.
Make caramel by heating the cane sugar with three tablespoonfuls of water.
When ready, spread the caramel on the bottom and sides of a deep cake tin.
Then boil the milk and cream with 80 g (2.8 oz) of sugar and the split and scraped vanilla pod.
Once infused, remove the vanilla pod and scrape it again to make sure you get all the aromatic black seeds.
Now add the semolina gradually and cook for 15 minutes on a low heat, stirring carefully.
Once the semolina is cooked, add the raisins, *Calvados* and then four egg yolks, carefully, one by one.
Whisk the two egg whites together until stiff and then add them, with the remaining 20 g (0.7 oz) of sugar, to the semolina mixture.
Mix all the ingredients together and then pour into the caramelised tin and bake for 35 minutes at 180-200°C (350-400°F/Gas mark 4-6).
Leave to cool and then turn out of the tin. Serve upside down so that the caramelised surface is showing and the caramel trickles down the sides.

Mont-Saint-Michel shortbread biscuits

Makes 50 biscuits

Preparation: 15 minutes
Cooking time: about 10 to 15 minutes

2 EGGS
120 G (4.2 OZ) CASTER SUGAR
30 G (1 OZ) BROWN SUGAR
480 G (1 LB) ALL PURPOSE FLOUR
230 G (8 OZ) UNSALTED BUTTER
30 G (1 OZ) SALTED BUTTER

Flavouring:
VANILLA OR CINNAMON

LEMON ZEST
50 ML (2 FL OZ) *CALVADOS*
PINCH OF SALT

Lightly whisk the eggs.
Add the caster sugar and a pinch of salt.
Mix well.
Add the sifted flour and mix again.
Turn the mixture out onto a work surface and make a well in the centre. Then add all the remaining ingredients – brown sugar, soft unsalted and salted butter, choice of flavouring, lemon zest and 50 ml (2 fl oz) of *Calvados*.
Knead thoroughly then leave to rest for 1 to 2 hours.
Roll out the dough with a rolling pin and then use a triangular cutter to make Mont-Saint-Michel shapes.
Glaze the biscuits with egg yolk and then bake for about 10 to 15 minutes at 160-180°C (325-350°F/Gas mark 3-4).

Mont-Saint-Michel shortbread biscuits

Summer Recipes

The summer sun warms the polders' rich soil which, in turn, produces tasty carrots, potatoes, asparagus, leeks and flavoured herbs.

Summer Starters

Garlic soup with toasted bread

Serves 4 to 8

Preparation: 30 minutes
Cooking time: about 1 hour

80 G (3 OZ) SPRING GARLIC, DEGERMED
400 G (14 OZ) SOUP POTATOES (BF 15 OR BINTJE)
200 G (7 OZ) CELERIAC
2 LITRES (3 1/2 PINTS) WATER
200 ML (7 FL OZ) CRÈME FRAÎCHE
A KNOB OF SALTED BUTTER
A FEW PIECES OF TOASTED BREAD, RUBBED WITH GARLIC

Peel the garlic and then peel and chop the potatoes and celeriac.
Bring the water to the boil, add all the vegetables and simmer for 1 hour, skimming off the foam regularly.
Once cooked, blend the soup in a blender or food processor.
Add the cream and butter and stir carefully.
Serve in small bowls with the bread.
The soup can be served both hot and cold.

Creamy mussel and celery soup

Serves 4 to 6

Preparation: 30 to 40 minutes
Cooking time: about 30 minutes

2 KG (4.4 LB) *BOUCHOT* MUSSELS, CLEANED
1 BOUQUET GARNI
3 CELERY STALKS, THINLY SLICED
40 G (1.5 OZ) ROUND GRAIN RICE
1 LITRE (1 3/4 PINTS) MILK
100 ML (3.5 FL OZ) DRY WHITE WINE
500 ML (17 FL OZ) DOUBLE CREAM, LIGHTLY WHIPPED
1 BUNCH OF PARSLEY OR CORIANDER
FRESHLY GROUND PEPPER

Heat the mussels in a pan with the white wine and bouquet garni.
Shake the pan until the mussels open and then remove from the heat.
Strain through a colander and keep the liquid.
Remove the mussels from their shells and set to one side.
Prepare the soup as follows: pour the mussel liquid and milk into a pan. Add the celery and rice and cook on a low heat for 30 minutes. Once cooked, blend the soup and strain it through a fine sieve. Thin the soup with a little milk, if necessary.
Check the seasoning.
Put the mussels in the bottom of bowls and then pour the creamy celery soup on top.
Pour the lightly whipped cream into the soup and garnish with parsley.
Add a twist of freshly ground pepper.

(Note: this soup does not need any salt, as the mussels already contain a sufficient amount to season this creamy soup.)

Creamy mussel and celery soup

Salmon tartare with herbs and spices

Serves 4

Preparation: 20 to 30 minutes

400 G (14 OZ) FRESH SALMON, BONED
1 SHALLOT, FINELY CHOPPED
A FEW PARSLEY, CURLY PARSLEY, CHERVIL, DILL, CHIVE AND CORIANDER LEAVES
1 TSP VIOLET MUSTARD
A PINCH OF DRIED SEAWEED
A PINCH OF CURRY, PAPRIKA AND MIXED SPICE
A DASH OF OLIVE OIL
JUICE OF 1 LIME
150 TO 200 G (5-7 OZ) PURSLANE OR SIMILAR LETTUCE
FRESHLY GROUND SALT AND PEPPER

Finely chop all the herbs and the shallot and mix them together.
Chop the salmon into small cubes.
When ready to serve, carefully mix the salmon with the herbs, spices, dried seaweed and mustard and then season with salt and pepper.
Arrange either in spoons or small piles on plates.
Drizzle with a few drops of lemon juice and olive oil.
Serve with a fresh summer lettuce (purslane or similar).

Salmon tartare with herbs and spices

Young rabbit pâté with *Pommeau* liqueur

Serves 6 to 8

Preparation: 40 minutes
Marinade: 40 minutes
Cooking time: 2 hours
(chill for 3 or 4 days before consuming)

1 RABBIT WEIGHING 1.5 KG TO 1.8 KG (3.3-4 LB)
500 G (1.1 LB) CHICKEN LIVER
500 G (1.1 LB) SAUSAGE MEAT
100 ML (3.5 FL OZ) *POMMEAU* LIQUEUR
+ SMALL GLASSFUL
1 EGG YOLK
1 ONION, CHOPPED
CHERVIL, THYME
BAY LEAVES
20 HAZELNUTS, WHOLE BUT PEELED
FRESHLY GROUND SALT AND PEPPER

Bone and coarsely chop the rabbit.
Chop the chicken liver and put in a large mixing bowl with 100 ml (3.5 fl oz) of *Pommeau* liqueur and marinate for 40 minutes.
Then add the sausage meat and egg yolk and mix.
Add the salt and pepper, onion, chopped chervil, thyme, half a bay leaf and the twenty hazelnuts.
Add a small glass of *Pommeau* liqueur and mix again.
Check the seasoning, then fill a terrine dish with the mixture.
Top with a sprig of thyme and a bay leaf, weigh down and cook for about 2 hours in the oven in a bain marie.
When cooked, remove from the oven, leave to cool and then chill for at least three or four days.
Serve with slices of farmhouse bread and a glass of *Pommeau* liqueur.

Melon and smoked ham salad

Serves 4

Preparation: 15 to 20 minutes

8 THIN SLICES OF SMOKED HAM
1 CURLY ENDIVE OR ESCAROLE LETTUCE
VINAIGRETTE MADE FROM WALNUT OIL,
WINE VINEGAR, SALT AND PEPPER
A FEW FRESH SHELLED WALNUTS
1 LARGE MELON, SLICED IN TWO
(RIPE AND SWEET)
A FEW TWISTS OF FRESHLY GROUND PEPPER
A FEW FRESH HERBS TO GARNISH

Cut the melon into quarters and scrape out the seeds. Using a melon baller, scoop out the fruit into balls.
Put the lettuce in a large salad bowl, drizzle with vinaigrette and mix.
Arrange the slices of smoked ham, melon balls and walnuts on the lettuce and garnish with fresh herbs.
Add a twist of freshly ground pepper and serve with slices of warm baguette.

Chive and tuna pâté

Serves 4

Preparation: 20 minutes
Cooking time: 35 minutes

80 G (3 OZ) TUNA FILLETS
1 BUNCH OF CHIVES, CHOPPED
1 KNOB OF BUTTER
200 ML (7 FL OZ) WARM WATER
10 G (0.35 OZ) GELATINE
1 CHIVE-FLAVOURED CREAM CHEESE, THINNED WITH LEMON JUICE
FRESHLY GROUND SALT AND PEPPER

Cut the tuna into long strips.
Finely chop the chives.
Melt the butter and add the warm water, gelatine, salt and pepper.
Arrange successive layers of chives and tuna strips, lengthways, in a terrine dish. When full, pour on the water and butter mixture.
Cover the terrine and bake at 180-200°C (350-400°F/Gas mark 4-6) in a bain maire for 35 minutes.
When cooked, leave to cool and then chill for 1 day.
Serve the pâté with the chive-flavoured cream cheese, thinned with lemon juice.

Chive and tuna pâté

Winkle parcels

Winkle parcels

Serves 4

Preparation: 20 to 30 minutes
Cooking time: 20 to 25 minutes, oven at 180°C (350°F/Gas mark 4)

500 G (1.1 LB) WINKLES, COOKED
400 G (14 OZ) PUFF PASTRY
100 G (3.5 OZ) DOUBLE CREAM
1 SHALLOT, FINELY CHOPPED
1 BUNCH OF PARSLEY, FINELY CHOPPED
2 EGG YOLKS
1 ADDITIONAL EGG YOLK, FOR THE PUFF PASTRY GLAZE
FRESHLY GROUND SALT AND PEPPER

Remove the winkles from their shells and mix with the double cream, shallot, two egg yolks, parsley, salt and pepper.
Roll out the puff pastry thinly and cut out eight circles of about 50 g (2 oz) each.
Divide the winkle and cream mixture up and place in the middle of each circle.
Glaze the edges of the pastry circles with a little egg yolk.
Fold and seal the circles as you would for apple turnovers.
Glaze the tops and lightly sprinkle with salt and pepper.
Bake for 20 to 25 minutes.
Serve hot with a small salad.

Normandy chicken salad

Normandy chicken salad

Serves 4

Preparation: 30 to 40 minutes
Cooking time: 20 minutes

2 FREE-RANGE CHICKEN BREASTS
6 LARGE PRUNES
500 ML (17 FL OZ) CHICKEN STOCK
4 SPOONFULS OF VINAIGRETTE MADE FROM GRAPESEED OIL AND CIDER VINEGAR
1 OR 2 CRUNCHY APPLES (CANADA OR REINE DES REINETTES), SLICED
200 G (7 OZ) MIXED LETTUCE
1 PINCH OF *GUÉRANDE* SEA SALT
1 BUNCH OF FRESH HERBS
FRESHLY GROUND SALT AND PEPPER

Prepare the chicken as follows the night before: split the breasts lengthwise, without fully separating them, then open them up flat.
Arrange the 6 chopped prunes in the centre of the chicken breasts.
Add salt and pepper and then roll the chicken breasts up, like sausages, with the prunes in the middle.
Use tin foil, cling film or clean tea towels to wrap them tight.
Simmer the chicken rolls in seasoned chicken stock for about 20 minutes.
Once cooked, chill in the liquid overnight.
The next day, unwrap the chicken rolls.
Mix the lettuce with most of the vinaigrette and arrange on four plates.
Thinly slice the chicken rolls and then place a slice of apple between each piece.
Arrange on the lettuce.
Drizzle over the rest of the vinaigrette and garnish with a few grains of *Guérande* sea salt and chopped fresh herbs.

Cockle and potato salad

Serves 4

Preparation: 30 minutes
Cooking time: 20 minutes

400 G (14 OZ) RATTE POTATOES
400 G (14 OZ) COCKLES, COOKED AND SHELLED
1 CURLY ENDIVE LETTUCE
A FEW FRESH HERBS, CHOPPED

For the vinaigrette:
JUICE OF 1 LEMON
2 SHALLOTS, FINELY CHOPPED
FRESH MIXED HERBS
OLIVE OIL
FRESHLY GROUND SALT AND PEPPER

Scrub and wash the potatoes and then cook them in salted water.
When cooked, peel while still warm.
Wash and dry the curly endive lettuce.
Put the lettuce in a salad bowl and mix with half of the vinaigrette.
Cut the potatoes into rounds and cook them over a high heat with the rest of the vinaigrette and the shelled cockles.
When ready, pour the cockles and potatoes onto the salad.
Garnish with a few fresh herbs and serve.

Summer Main Courses

Summer saddle of lamb

Serves 4

Preparation: 15 minutes for the saddle of lamb + 20 to 25 minutes for the vegetables
Cooking time: 30 minutes for the saddle

800 G TO 1 KG (1.8-2.2 LB) SALT-MEADOW SADDLE OF LAMB
4 GARLIC CLOVES
4 SMALL SHALLOTS
4 RIPE TOMATOES, QUARTERED
20 G (0.7 OZ) BUTTER
1 GLASS OF WATER
A FEW SUMMER VEGETABLES, COOKED (PEAS, ASPARAGUS, GREEN BEANS, TURNIPS, CARROTS, ETC.)
FRESHLY GROUND SALT AND PEPPER

Preheat the oven to 180°C (350°F/Gas mark 4).
Put the lamb saddle in a lightly buttered oven-proof dish and cook for about 20 minutes, until brown on all sides.
Then add the unpeeled garlic cloves, unpeeled shallots and tomatoes.
Season with salt and pepper, add a glass of water and continue cooking for another 10 minutes, basting regularly.
Once cooked, cut the lamb into slices and arrange on a serving dish with the summer vegetables.
Pour on the gravy and serve.

Mustard baked cod

Serves 4

Preparation: 30 minutes
Cooking time: 5 to 6 minutes

4 COD FILLETS, WEIGHING 150 G (5 OZ) EACH WITH SKIN
2 SPOONFULS OF WHOLE-GRAIN MUSTARD
1 TSP STRONG MUSTARD
SOME BREADCRUMBS
1 SHALLOT, CHOPPED
1 BUNCH OF PARSLEY, CHOPPED
1 EGG
8 BAY LEAVES
30 G (1 OZ) UNSALTED BUTTER
1 GLASS OF CIDER
300 ML (1/2 PINT) CREAM
1 SPOONFUL OF FLOUR
200 G (7 OZ) MANGETOUT, BOILED
FRESHLY GROUND SALT AND PEPPER

Season the cod fillets with salt and pepper and then lightly dust the skin with flour.
Lightly beat the egg and then dip the skin side of the fillets into the egg.
Mix the whole-grain mustard with the breadcrumbs, parsley and shallot and then coat the skin side of the cod with this mixture.
Press a bay leaf into the mixture on the fillets.
Melt the butter in a non-stick pan and fry the four cod fillets skin side down for 4 minutes, until the skin is crispy.
Flip the cod fillets and fry the other side for 2 minutes.
Meanwhile, reduce the cider and strong mustard in a pan until syrupy.
Then add the cream and reduce again until the sauce has the same syrupy consistency.
Season with salt and pepper.
Serve the cod skin side up, with the sauce and some mangetout, steamed in butter.

Summer saddle of lamb

Baked sea bream with savory

Serves 4

Preparation: 15 to 20 minutes
Cooking time: 20 to 30 minutes at 160°C (325°F/Gas mark 3)

1 sea bream, weighing 1.2 kg (2.7 lb)
4 ripe tomatoes, cut into quarters
1 onion, sliced
1 shallot, chopped
1 glass of cider
1 lemon, sliced
50 ml (1.7 fl oz) olive oil
100 g (3.5 oz) butter
A few sprigs of savory
Freshly ground salt and pepper

Scale, trim and gut the sea bream and then wash and dry.
Place the sliced onion, shallot, a few sprigs of savory and cider in an oven-proof dish.
Then put the sea bream in the middle of the dish with the tomato quarters around it and drizzle with half the olive oil.
Insert more sprigs of savory into the gutted head and body of the sea bream.
Place a few slices of lemon on top of the fish and drizzle on the rest of the olive oil.
Pop the fish into the preheated oven and bake for 20 to 30 minutes.
Check the sea bream about halfway through cooking. If it is already brown, cover with a sheet of tin foil and continue cooking, basting every 5 minutes.
Spread the butter over the sea bream, season with salt and pepper and serve.

Baked sea bream with savory

Locally caught mackerel in thyme and salt

Locally caught mackerel in thyme and salt

Serves 4

Preparation: 10 minutes
Cooking time: 15 to 20 minutes, oven at 200-220°C (400-450°F Gas mark 6-8)

8 MACKEREL
1.2 KG TO 1.5 KG (2.7-3.3 LB) COARSE GREY SEA SALT
2 BUNCHES OF FRESH THYME
4 BAY LEAVES
A FEW TWISTS OF FRESHLY GROUND PEPPER
SOME POTATOES, BOILED

Sauce:
100 G (3.5 OZ) DOUBLE CREAM
FRESHLY GROUND SALT AND PEPPER

Gut the mackerel, rinse in cold water and pat dry.
Mix the sea salt, fresh thyme, ground pepper and bay leaves together.
Spread half this mixture in an oven-proof dish and place the mackerel on top, side by side.
Then evenly cover the mackerel with the rest of the sea salt mixture and bake for 15 to 20 minutes.
Meanwhile, lightly season the double cream with salt and pepper and heat until it starts to thin.
Remove the mackerel from the oven and break the salt crust.
Brush the remaining salt off the fish and arrange two on each plate.
Drizzle with the warm double cream and serve with boiled potatoes.

Saddle of rabbit with lemon

Serves 4

Preparation: 20 minutes
Cooking time: 1 1/2 hours

2 SMALL SADDLES OF FARMHOUSE RABBIT
2 LONG SHALLOTS
2 GARLIC CLOVES
2 SPRIGS OF LEMON THYME
40 G (1.5 OZ) BUTTER
1 SPOONFUL OF PEANUT OIL
2 JUICY LEMONS
1 SPOONFUL OF FLOUR
FRESHLY GROUND SALT AND PEPPER

Slice a lemon in two and rub it all over the rabbit.
Season with salt and pepper.
Using a small sieve, lightly dust the rabbit with flour.
Then finely chop the shallots, crush the garlic and squeeze the juice from the second lemon.
Heat the butter and oil in a casserole and add the shallots and garlic.
Add the rabbit and brown on all sides.
Then cover with water and lemon juice and season with the sprig of lemon, thyme, salt and pepper and cook for 1 1/2 hours on a low heat.
Baste regularly and add a little water if it starts to dry out.
About halfway through cooking (45 minutes) turn the rabbit over.
Serve hot with the gravy.

Salt-baked squab with fresh thyme

Serves 4

Preparation: 45 minutes to 1 hour
Cooking time: 30 minutes

4 SQUABS
5 OR 6 SPRIGS OF FRESH THYME
3 TO 4 KG (6.6-8.8 LB) COARSE SEA SALT
A PINCH OF PEPPER
SEASONAL VEGETABLES

Gravy:
2 ONIONS
1 CARROT
2 GARLIC CLOVES
2 SHALLOTS
1 BOUQUET GARNI
3 TOMATOES
OLIVE OIL
SALT

Ask your butcher to prepare the squabs, saving you the giblets (gizzards, hearts, heads and livers) and cutting the pinions and necks in two.
Make some gravy with the giblets and gravy ingredients, then sieve.
Then mix the sea salt with the sprigs of thyme.
Fry the squabs in a little oil until nicely browned.
Spread half the sea salt and thyme mixture in a large oven-proof dish, lay the squabs on top, season with pepper and then cover completely with the rest of the mixture.
Bake at 200-220°C (400-450°F/Gas mark 6-8) for 15 to 20 minutes, depending on how you like the meat done.
Remove from the oven, break the salt crust and brush off any remaining bits of salt.
Serve hot with the gravy.
This dish can be served with seasonal vegetables, such as asparagus or fresh peas.

Saddle of rabbit with lemon

Stone-baked sea bass

Stone-baked sea bass

Serves 4

Preparation: 30 minutes
Cooking time: 1 hour

1 sea bass, weighing 1.5 to 2 kg (3.3-4.4 lb)
Salt and pepper
Olive oil
1 tsp strong mustard
4 or 5 tbsp double cream
A knob of butter
Roughly mashed potatoes
3 or 4 flat stones

Heat up the stones for 2 or 3 days in the embers of a fire before making the dish.
On the day, gut – but don't scale – the sea bass and then dip in olive oil.
Remove the hot stones from the fire, arrange in the bottom of an oven-proof dish and position the sea bass on top.
Pop in the oven to cook at 200°C (400°F/Gas mark 6) for 1 hour, checking regularly.
Turn the sea bass over halfway through cooking so it cooks on both sides.
While the fish is cooking, make a sauce by heating the cream, mustard, salt, pepper and butter in a pan for a few minutes.
Serve the sea bass on the hot stones accompanied by the sauce and mashed potatoes.

Brittany fish chowder with mixed spices

Ask your fishmonger for 1 kg (2.2 lb) of assorted fish fillets for four people.
Wash the vegetables, cut into large pieces and lightly fry in a little butter.
Then cover the vegetables with water, a little wine or cider, the oil and vinegar.
Season, sprinkle with a little of the mixed spices and cook on a low heat.
When the vegetables are cooked, add the assorted fish fillets and cook for 7 to 8 minutes.
Serve with the stock and garnish with the chopped herbs.

Serves 4

Preparation: 30 minutes
Cooking time: 30 to 40 minutes

3 TO 6 ASSORTED FISH FILLETS, DEPENDING ON PERSONAL TASTE AND AVAILABILITY (GURNARD, MACKEREL, WHITING, SURMULLET, SEA BREAM, PLAICE, BRILL, JOHN DORY, ETC.)
2 OR 3 ONIONS
2 LARGE CELERY STALKS
1 BOUQUET GARNI
2 OR 3 LARGE POTATOES
50 G (2 OZ) BUTTER
2 CARROTS
2 LEEKS
2 GARLIC CLOVES
3 SHALLOTS
A MIX OF 5 OR 6 SPICES (PEPPER, NUTMEG, CLOVES, SAFFRON, JUNIPER, MIXED SPICE, ETC.)
100 ML (3.5 FL OZ) OLIVE OIL
1 SMALL COURGETTE
300 ML (1/2 PINT) WHITE WINE OR CIDER
1 TBSP VINEGAR
2 OR 3 TBSP FINELY CHOPPED HERBS (PARSLEY, CHIVES, CHERVIL)
FRESHLY GROUND SALT AND PEPPER

Brittany fish chowder with mixed spices

Summer Desserts

Red berry and mint desserts

Serves 4

Preparation: 25 minutes the night before, 5 minutes on the day

Depending on availability:

1 SMALL PUNNET OF STRAWBERRIES
1 SMALL PUNNET OF RASPBERRIES
1 SMALL PUNNET OF BLACKBERRIES
1 SMALL PUNNET OF REDCURRANTS
1 SMALL PUNNET OF BLACKCURRANTS
500 ML (17 FL OZ) WARM SYRUP
1 BUNCH OF FRESH MINT, CHOPPED
1 TBSP BLACKBERRY LIQUEUR
50 G (2 OZ) CASTER SUGAR
FROMAGE BLANC ICE CREAM

Wash and hull the strawberries, raspberries, blackberries, redcurrants, blackcurrants, etc.
Cut the larger fruit into cubes and leave the smaller fruit, like the currants, whole.
Make the syrup by boiling 500 ml (17 fl oz) of water with 500 g (1.1 lb) of sugar and then cool to 30°C (86°F).
Then put the fruit in a mixing bowl and pour in the warm syrup.
Add the blackberry liqueur, chopped fresh mint and caster sugar, and marinate for one day, or overnight, in the fridge.
The next day, drain the fruit and arrange it in round rings.
Decorate with the mint leaves and a few whole fruits.
Turn out of the rings, arrange on plates and drizzle with the chilled marinade syrup.
Serve with fromage blanc ice cream.

Cherry clafoutis

Serves 4

Preparation: 30 minutes
Cooking time: 30 minutes

100 ML (3.5 FL OZ) SINGLE CREAM
100 ML (3.5 FL OZ) MILK
2 LARGE EGGS
120 G (4.2 OZ) FLOUR, SIFTED
20 G (0.7 OZ) BUTTER
100 G (3.5 OZ) BROWN SUGAR
20 G (0.7 OZ) CASTER SUGAR
450 G (1 LB) CHERRIES (BIGARREAU IF POSSIBLE)

Whisk the eggs with the brown sugar and then fold in the sifted flour.
Then add the melted butter and pour in the single cream and milk.
Remove the cherry stalks and stones, then grease an oven-proof dish and fill it with the cherries. Pour the mixture on top and bake at 180°C (350°F/Gas mark 4) for 30 minutes.
Remove from the oven and dust with caster sugar.

Red berry and mint desserts

Small dark chocolate cakes

Small dark chocolate cakes

Serves 6 to 8

Preparation: 20 minutes
Cooking time: 12 minutes

100 G (3.5 OZ) PLAIN CHOCOLATE
20 G (0.7 OZ) COCOA POWDER
100 G (3.5 OZ) BUTTER
90 G (3.2 OZ) ICING SUGAR
40 G (1.5 OZ) FLOUR
2 OR 3 EGGS, DEPENDING ON THEIR SIZE

Melt the butter and chocolate in a bain marie, then add the cocoa.
Whisk the eggs and sugar in a mixing bowl, then fold in the flour.
Then mix in the melted chocolate and leave to rest for 1 hour.
Pour the mixture into individual, greased and floured tins and bake for 12 minutes at 180°C (350°F/Gas mark 4).
Warm in the oven for a couple of minutes before serving.

Normandy tartlets

Serves 4

Preparation: 20 minutes
Cooking time: 20 minutes

3 TO 6 NORMANDY APPLES (DEPENDING ON THEIR SIZE)
300 G (10.5 OZ) PUFF PASTRY
1 LEMON
10 G (0.35 OZ) BUTTER
CINNAMON
2 TBSP CLEAR HONEY
CALVADOS
ICING SUGAR

Preheat the oven to 200-220°C (400-450°F/Gas mark 6-8).
Roll out the puff pastry, cut out four 15 to 18 cm (6-7") circles and place on a greased baking sheet.
Peel and core the apples.
Grate the lemon zest and squeeze out the juice.
Cut the apples into slices and pour some lemon juice over them.
Mix the rest of the lemon juice with the honey.
Arrange the apple slices in a star shape on the pastry circles and brush with the lemon and honey juice.
Then mix the grated lemon zest with the cinnamon and sprinkle over the tartlets.
Pop in the oven and bake for 20 minutes.
Turn out of the tins using a spatula and transfer to a rack to cool.
Serve warm.
They can be flambed with *Calvados* or dusted with icing sugar.

Bergamot crème brûlée

Bergamot crème brûlée

Serves 8

Preparation: 25 minutes
Cooking time: 45 minutes

500 ML (17 FL OZ) SINGLE CREAM
500 ML (17 FL OZ) MILK
2 VANILLA PODS
9 EGG YOLKS
150 G (5 OZ) CASTER SUGAR
80 G (3 OZ) LIGHT BROWN SUGAR
20 G (0.7 OZ) BERGAMOT OR CARDAMOM

Split and scrape out the vanilla pods, roughly chop the bergamot and put them in a pan with the milk and cream.
Bring to the boil and then cover with a tea towel and lid. Leave to infuse for about 1 hour and then filter the mixture through a fine sieve.
Preheat the oven to 100°C (200°F/Gas mark 1/4).
Mix the egg yolks and caster sugar in a mixing bowl without beating.
Gradually add the milk and cream mixture, mixing with a wooden spoon.
Sieve the cream again and then pour into eight white porcelain crème brûlée dishes and bake for 45 minutes.
Check to see if they are properly cooked by lightly shaking the dishes. The centres should be firm, not runny.
Cool the crèmes down to room temperature, then pop in the fridge for 4 hours.
Just before serving, sprinkle with some brown sugar and caramelise the tops lightly under the grill.

Blackcurrant roasted peaches

Serves 4

Preparation: 15 minutes
Cooking time: 30 minutes

4 LARGE WHITE OR WILD PEACHES
100 G (3.5 OZ) LIGHT BROWN SUGAR
50 G (2 OZ) BLACKCURRANTS
500 ML (17 FL OZ) *BEAUJOLAIS* RED WINE
50 G (2 OZ) UNSALTED BUTTER
VANILLA ICE CREAM

Choose four ripe peaches.
Use small pliers to pinch the stone and remove it with a quick twist of your wrist.
Then fill the hole with the blackcurrants, butter and sugar and put the peaches in an oven-proof dish.
Add the *Beaujolais* red wine and bake at 180°C (350°F/Gas mark 4) for 30 minutes.
Turn the peaches every 10 minutes, basting regularly. To check whether the peaches are cooked, prick with a knife. If it goes in easily and the skin peels off, they are cooked.
Serve hot with a scoop of vanilla ice cream.

Mont-Saint-Michel biscuits with jam from the bay

Makes about 50 biscuits

Preparation: 30 minutes
Cooking time: about 12 to 15 minutes

300 G (10.5 OZ) FLOUR
2 EGGS
2 EGG YOLKS
160 G (5.6 OZ) CASTER SUGAR
170 G (6 OZ) BUTTER, CUT INTO PIECES
A PINCH OF SALT
ZEST OF 1 LEMON
A PINCH OF CINNAMON

Make a well in the flour on your pastry board and fill it with the sugar and eggs. Carefully mix the eggs and sugar with your fingertips, incorporating the flour little by little. Then add the softened butter pieces, salt, lemon zest and cinnamon. Knead the dough for about 2 or 3 minutes (don't overwork it).
Make it into a ball, leave to rest for a while, then roll it out to the desired thickness.
Use a cutter or knife to cut out the biscuits then glaze with the egg yolks.
Dust with a little sugar and spice and bake at 150°C (300°F/Gas mark 2) for about 12 to 15 minutes.

Bay of Mont-Saint-Michel jam

To make the jam:
1 KG (2.2 LB) BLACKBERRIES
750 G (1.65 LB) GRANULATED SUGAR
JUICE OF 1 LEMON
250 ML (9 FL OZ) MINERAL WATER

Sort the blackberries, rinse in cold water, drain in a colander and pat dry with a tea towel.
Pour the water and sugar into a jam pan. Heat and crystallise, stirring with a wooden spoon.
Use a sugar thermometer to keep the temperature at 115°C (250°F). To test, run your hands under cold water and then roll a little of the mixture in your hand. It should feel like modelling clay.
Then add the blackberries and lemon juice. Mix carefully and simmer for 5 or 6 minutes, stirring occasionally.
When the syrup thickens and the fruit is no longer on the surface, the jam is ready. The temperature should be 105°C (225°F) on the sugar thermometer.
This recipe will make about 5 pots of 300 g (10.5 oz).

Mont-Saint-Michel biscuits with jam from the bay

Pan-fried blackberries with vanilla ice cream

Pan-fried blackberries with vanilla ice cream

Serves 4

Preparation: 20 minutes
Cooking time: 5 minutes

800 G (1.8 LB) BLACKBERRIES
200 ML (7 FL OZ) BLACKBERRY LIQUEUR
100 G (3.5 OZ) SUGAR
4 GENEROUS SCOOPS OF VANILLA ICE CREAM
400 ML (13.5 FL OZ) CUSTARD

Cook the blackberries, sugar and blackberry liqueur in a non-stick pan on a high heat for 4 or 5 minutes. The blackberries are ready when they are hot in the centre.
Pour the blackberries and sauce into four porcelain dishes and top with a generous scoop of ice cream.
Drizzle with custard and serve.

Normandy coconut tart

Serves 6 to 8

Preparation: 20 to 30 minutes
Cooking time: 30 minutes

500 G (1.1 LB) SWEET PASTRY
100 G (3.5 OZ) ICING SUGAR
20 G (0.7 OZ) GROUND ALMONDS
20 G (0.7 OZ) GROUND HAZELNUTS
50 G (2 OZ) DESICCATED COCONUT
5 G (1/8 OZ) CORN FLOUR
60 G (2.1 OZ) BUTTER
1 EGG
1 TSP *CALVADOS*
150 G (5 OZ) SINGLE CREAM
50 G (2 OZ) COARSE SUGAR (TO DECORATE)

Roll out the sweet pastry and use to line a flan dish. Prick with a fork and then chill.
Preheat the oven to 180°C (350°F/Gas mark 4).
Then prepare the coconut cream. Mix the icing sugar, ground almonds and hazelnuts, coconut and corn flour and then sift.
Work the butter in a mixing bowl until soft and then add the coconut mixture and the egg.
Mix the ingredients together and pour in the *Calvados.* Add the single cream and when the mixture is smooth, pour it into the pastry case.
Bake for 30 minutes.
Remove from the oven and sprinkle with the coarse sugar.
Leave to cool and then serve.

Baked custard with nougat

Serves 6 to 8

Preparation: 25 minutes
Cooking time: 40 minutes

300 ML (1/2 PINT) MILK
300 ML (1/2 PINT) SINGLE CREAM
140 G (4.5 OZ) CASTER SUGAR
6 TO 8 EGG YOLKS, DEPENDING ON SIZE
50 G (2 OZ) HARD NOUGAT (PREFERABLY FROM MONTÉLIMAR) FINELY CHOPPED

Make the custard with the milk, single cream, sugar and egg yolks.
When the custard is ready, add the nougat.
Pour the mixture into a 20 cm (8") diameter Charlotte tin and cook in the oven in a bain marie at 180°C (350°F/Gas mark 4) for about 40 minutes.
Check to see if the cake is cooked by inserting a knife into the centre. If the blade comes out clean, the cake is ready.
Turn out of the tin when cold and place on a serving dish, decorated with chopped nougat.

Autumn Recipes

Autumn marks the start of the scallop fishing season in Granville harbour while, on the other side of the bay, Cancale's stake-grown mussels and flesh oysters are at their very best.

PROPRIETE
INALIENABLE

Autumn Starters

Serves 4 to 8

Preparation: 40 minutes
Cooking time: 1.5 hours

1 PUMPKIN (APPROX. 1.5 KG OR 3.3 LB)
2 SHALLOTS
2 ONIONS
1 LEEK
30 G (1 OZ) BUTTER
500 ML (17 FL OZ) CHICKEN STOCK
1 LITRE FULL CREAM MILK
1 LARGE POTATO
(BF 15 OR BINTJE)
1 SPOONFUL OF CREAM
1 TSP SUGAR
1 BUNCH OF CHERVIL
FRESHLY GROUND SALT AND PEPPER
BEAUFORT CHEESE SHAVINGS

Creamy pumpkin and chervil soup

Peel the pumpkin, scrape out the seeds and fibres and cut the flesh into large chunks.
Peel and finely chop the shallots, onions and leek.
Thoroughly rinse all these vegetables.
Melt the butter in a pan or casserole over a medium heat and then lightly fry the shallots, onions and leek.
Then add the pumpkin and sweat for 5 minutes over a very low heat, stirring regularly.
Add a teaspoon of sugar.
Season with salt and pepper and steam for 5 to 6 minutes.
Meanwhile, peel and roughly chop the potato and add to the pan.
At this point, add the milk and chicken stock. Then cover and cook for about 1 hour.
When cooked, blend in a blender or food processor. Sieve the soup through a fine sieve and then add a spoonful of cream.
Check the seasoning and serve hot.
Garnish this creamy soup with a few Beaufort or Cantal cheese shavings and a handful of chervil leaves.

Serves 4 to 6

Preparation: 30 minutes
Resting time: 3 hours
Cooking time: 30 to 40 minutes at 180-200°C (350-400°F/Gas mark 4-6)

400 G (14 OZ) RED ONIONS
2 EGG YOLKS
5 TBSP THICK FARMHOUSE CREAM
200 G (7 OZ) FLOUR
180 G (6.3 OZ) BUTTER
1 PINCH OF NUTMEG
4 TBSP SINGLE CREAM
FRESHLY GROUND SALT AND PEPPER

Saint-Michel onion tart

Put the flour, 100 g (3.5 oz) of soft butter, a pinch of salt and four tablespoons of single cream in a bowl.
Rub in the ingredients to form a dough. Knead into a ball, wrap in a tea towel and leave the pastry to rest for 3 hours.
Meanwhile, peel and finely chop the red onions and then lightly fry in 50 g (2 oz) of butter. Season with salt and pepper.
Cook the onions for about ten minutes until soft and golden.
Preheat the oven to 180-200°C (350-400°F/Gas mark 4-6).
Grease a flan tin, roll out the pastry and then line the tin with the pastry.
Mix the egg yolks and cream together in another bowl and season with salt, pepper and a pinch of nutmeg.
Arrange the onions in the pastry case, pour on the cream mixture and then bake for 30 to 40 minutes.

Creamy pumpkin and chervil soup

Chicory and crab claw salad

Chicory and crab claw salad

Serves 4

Preparation: 30 to 40 minutes
Cooking time: 15 to 20 minutes

2 LARGE CRABS
4 HEADS OF CHICORY
8 SPOONFULS OF VINAIGRETTE MADE FROM WALNUT OIL, RASPBERRY VINEGAR, LEMON JUICE, SALT AND PEPPER
A FEW CHERVIL OR FRESH HERB LEAVES TO GARNISH
1 BOUQUET GARNI
FRESHLY GROUND SALT AND PEPPER

Boil the crabs in a seasoned court-bouillon (salt, pepper and the bouquet garni) for 15 to 20 minutes (depending on the size).
When cooked, drain and carefully remove the creamy body meat and flaky white meat from the claws and legs.
Remove the outer chicory leaves and arrange on plates in a star shape.
Finely chop the chicory hearts and mix with four spoonfuls of vinaigrette and the creamy crab meat.
Roughly chop the claw meat and arrange over the chicory leaves.
Drizzle with the chicory and crab vinaigrette and garnish with a few chervil leaves.

Scallops and polder-grown carrots

Serves 4

Preparation: 30 minutes
Cooking time: 6 minutes

4 LARGE POLDER-GROWN CARROTS
8 TO 12 LARGE SCALLOPS
1 LITRE FISH STOCK
2 TBSP DOUBLE CREAM
1 LARGE SPOONFUL OF MELTED BUTTER
4 GENEROUS HANDFULS OF ROCK SAMPHIRE
200 ML (7 FL OZ) VINAIGRETTE MADE FROM SALT, PEPPER, OLIVE OIL AND CIDER VINEGAR
200 G (7 OZ) LETTUCE (LAMBS' LETTUCE, ENDIVE, PURSLANE OR RADICCHIO)
A FEW FRESHLY PICKED HERBS TO GARNISH
4 X 8-10 CM (3-4 INCH) TINS
FRESHLY GROUND SALT AND PEPPER

Peel and then boil the carrots whole in the fish stock, being careful not to overcook them. Then drain. (If you do not have any fish stock, you can simply cook the carrots in water.)
Gently heat the cream in a small pan with some salt and pepper.
Slice the scallops and cut the carrots into rounds.
Arrange a little rock samphire in the base of the tins and then alternate between scallop and carrot slices until the tin is full.
Add a little butter, season with salt and pepper and then pop into a hot oven for 5 to 6 minutes.
Turn out onto warm plates and pour on the melted cream. Serve with lettuce and rock samphire and garnish with the vinaigrette and fresh herbs.

Scallops and polder-grown carrots

Scallop and mushroom pie

Scallop and mushroom pie

Serves 4 to 6

Preparation: 30 minutes
Cooking time: 30 minutes

500 G (1.1 LB) PUFF PASTRY
12 SCALLOPS WITH ROE
80 G (2.8 OZ) BUTTER
2 SHALLOTS
1 BUNCH OF FRESH HERBS
250 G (9 OZ) FIELD MUSHROOMS
(CEPS, CHANTERELLES, PIEDS-DE-MOUTONS, ETC.)
80 G (2.8 OZ) CRÈME FRAÎCHE
3 EGG YOLKS
FRESHLY GROUND SALT AND PEPPER

Roll out half the pastry and use to line a flan tin, then chill.
Meanwhile, sweat the two chopped shallots in the butter.
Add the fresh herbs and chopped mushrooms, simmer for a few minutes and then drain.
Mix the crème fraîche and egg yolks with the mushroom mixture.
Season with salt and pepper and leave to cool.
Pour half of the mixture into the pastry case.
Cover with the seasoned scallops, cut into two, and top with the rest of the mushroom mixture.
Roll out the remaining pastry to a circle for the lid and then seal the pie.
Make a hole in the centre of the lid and then glaze with the third egg yolk.
Bake at 200°C (400°F/Gas mark 6) for about 30 minutes.
Leave to rest a little once cooked and then serve.

Sausage and potato slices with tartare sauce

Serves 4

Preparation: 30 minutes
Cooking time: 1 hour

1 SAUSAGE, RAW AND LIGHTLY SMOKED, WEIGHING 500 TO 600 G (1.1-1.3 LB)
2 ONIONS
1 CARROT
1 BOUQUET GARNI
8 ROSEVAL POTATOES
250 ML (9 FL OZ) MAYONNAISE
2 GHERKINS
2 CAPERS
1 SMALL BUNCH OF PARSLEY
JUICE OF 1 LEMON
1 SHALLOT
A FEW SPRIGS OF TARRAGON
A FEW FRESH HERB LEAVES
1 TOMATO
FRESHLY GROUND SALT AND PEPPER

To cook the sausage: make a court-bouillon with the onions, carrot, bouquet garni and a little salt. Bring to a simmer and add the sausage.
After 30 minutes, add the potatoes, complete with skins. Cook for about another 30 minutes. Then drain the sausage and potatoes and peel the potatoes while still hot.
Leave to cool while making the tartare sauce: mix the mayonnaise with the two finely chopped gherkins, capers, chopped parsley, lemon juice, chopped shallot, chopped tarragon leaves, salt, pepper and the peeled and finely chopped tomato.
Arrange the warm sausage slices and warm potato slices in turn on each plate.
Garnish with a few fresh herb leaves and serve with the tartare sauce on the side.

Serves 4

Preparation: 30 minutes
Resting time: 1 hour
Cooking time: a few minutes

200 G (7 OZ) SIFTED FLOUR
2 EGG WHITES
1 PINCH OF BAKING POWDER
1 SPOONFUL OF OLIVE OIL
SALT
MIXED PEPPERCORNS
1 OR 2 CAMEMBERT CHEESES (DEPENDING ON APPETITE AND MENU)
250 ML (9 FL OZ) LOCAL BEER

Camembert and mixed peppercorn fritters

Batter: sift the flour into a bowl. Add the baking powder, oil, pinch of salt, ground mixed pepper and beer.

Mix well and leave to rest for 1 hour.

When the hour is up, whisk the egg whites with a pinch of salt until stiff and then fold into the batter mixture.

Be careful not to overwork the batter.

Heat the fryer to 170°C (325°F/Gas mark 3).

Cut the Camembert into eight pieces.

Dip each piece into the batter and then fry in the hot oil for a few minutes.

Serve these Camembert fritters with a side salad (curly endive, escarole or lambs' lettuce).

Camembert and mixed peppercorn fritters

Free-range chicken and Normandy duck foie gras parcels

Free-range chicken and Normandy duck *foie gras* parcels

Serves 4

Preparation the night before: 30 minutes

Cooking time: 12 to 15 minutes

1 LARGE FREE-RANGE CHICKEN BREAST
1 LITRE (1 3/4 PINTS) CHICKEN STOCK
100 G (3.5 OZ) RAW *FOIE GRAS*
1 PINCH OF *GUÉRANDE* SEA SALT AND FRESHLY GROUND PEPPER
MIXED FRESH HERBS
100 G (3.5 OZ) BABY FRENCH BEANS, COOKED *AL DENTE*
100 G (3.5 OZ) GREEN ASPARAGUS SPEARS, COOKED *AL DENTE*
200 ML (7 FL OZ) VINAIGRETTE MADE FROM OLIVE OIL, CIDER VINEGAR AND BALSAMIC VINEGAR

The night before, cut a pocket into the middle of the chicken breast. Stuff the pocket with 100 g (3.5 oz) of raw *foie gras*. Season well and then wrap tightly in several layers of cling film to form a sausage shape.
Heat the chicken stock. When it starts to boil, add the chicken breast. Bring back to the boil and then turn off the heat and cover the pan. Leave to rest for 12 to 15 minutes depending on the size of the breast.
Drain and when cool, place in the fridge.
The next day, gently warm the vegetables in a little vinaigrette. Remove the cling film from the chicken breast and cut into even slices.
Arrange the chicken parcels and warm vegetables on large plates, garnish with fresh herbs and drizzle with the warm vinaigrette.
Season with freshly ground pepper and a pinch of Guérande sea salt.
Alternatively serve with a watercress and fresh herb salad.

Autumn Main Courses

Garlic breaded monkfish

Serves 4

Preparation: 30 minutes
Cooking time: 20 minutes

4 small monkfish tails weighing 200 to 250 g (7-9 oz)
4 small sprigs of wild thyme
100 ml (3.5 fl oz) olive oil
50 g (2 oz) butter + 80 g (3 oz) for the sauce
8 garlic cloves
1 pinch of saffron
100 g (3.5 oz) breadcrumbs
1 glass of white wine
1 egg
1 bunch of parsley to garnish
Freshly ground salt and pepper

Degerm and chop four garlic cloves. Strip the wild thyme and mix the leaves with the garlic, breadcrumbs and a little salt and pepper.
Dip the monkfish tails in the lightly beaten egg and then sprinkle on the breadcrumb topping and saffron.
Heat 50 g (2 oz) of butter and 100 ml (3.5 fl oz) of olive oil in a non-stick pan.
Fry the remaining four garlic cloves whole, complete with their skins.
When the cloves are golden brown, add the four monkfish tails and fry for 20 minutes over a high heat, being careful not to let them burn.
Turn and baste regularly.
Once the monkfish is cooked, remove from the pan.
Deglaze the pan with the white wine, leave to reduce and add the 80 g (3 oz) of butter at the end.
Serve the monkfish tails hot with the sauce on the side. Garnish with parsley.

Skate with caper butter

Serves 4

Preparation: 20 minutes
Cooking time: 30 minutes for the court-bouillon,
10 minutes for the skate wings

4 skate wings, weighing about 200 g (7 oz)
100 g (3.5 oz) small capers
120 g (4.2 oz) butter
Juice of 1 lemon
1 bunch of parsley
2 shallots, peeled
2 carrots
1 glass of cider
1 onion, studded with cloves
1 bouquet garni
1 spoonful of cider vinegar
Freshly ground salt and pepper

Make a court-bouillon with the carrots, onion, bouquet garni, cider vinegar, cider, salt, pepper and water.
Leave to infuse for about thirty minutes.
Add the skate wings and simmer for about ten minutes.
Drain the skate and then pat dry with kitchen paper.
Remove the skin and cartilage and arrange in a small dish.
Then melt the butter in a small pan and add the lemon juice, capers, parsley leaves and finely chopped shallots.
Season the butter with salt and pepper and then pour over the skate wings.
Serve straight away.

The butter should be light brown in colour but not burnt.

Garlic breaded monkfish

Pan-fried salmon and field mushrooms

Serves 4

Preparation: 30 minutes
Cooking time: 5 minutes for the salmon steaks,
5 minutes for the mushrooms,
5 minutes for the sauce

4 SALMON STEAKS WITH SKIN, WEIGHING 150 G (5 OZ)
4 BAY LEAVES
80 G (2.8 OZ) SALTED BUTTER
1 GLASS OF CIDER
400 G (14 OZ) FIELD MUSHROOMS (CEPS, CHANTERELLES, MEADOW MUSHROOMS, ETC.), WASHED
4 PINCHES OF GUÉRANDE SEA SALT
FRESHLY GROUND PEPPER

Make a small slit in the skin of each salmon steak and insert a bay leaf.
Melt the butter in a non-stick pan and pan-fry the salmon steaks, skin side down, for 4 minutes.
Then turn the steaks and fry the other side for 1 to 2 minutes. Remove the steaks from the pan and keep warm.
In the same butter, fry the mushrooms (the ceps and chanterelles can be sliced but not the meadow mushrooms) over a high heat for about 5 minutes.
Remove the mushrooms and deglaze the pan using the cider.
Reduce the liquid until syrupy.
Arrange the warm salmon steaks on plates, skin side up, with a bay leaf on each one.
Add the mushrooms and pour over the cider sauce.
Top each steak with a pinch of *Guérande* sea salt and a twist of pepper.

Pan-fried salmon and field mushrooms

Normandy-style quails with long shallots

Normandy-style quails with long shallots

Serves 4

Preparation: 15 minutes
Cooking time: about 20 minutes

4 QUAILS
50 G (2 OZ) BUTTER
200 G (7 OZ) LONG SHALLOTS
50 G (2 OZ) CHOPPED BACON
1 GLASS OF *POMMEAU* LIQUEUR
A FEW SHAVINGS OF FRESH TRUFFLE
FRESHLY GROUND SALT AND PEPPER

Melt the butter in a casserole and brown the quails on all sides over a high heat with the unpeeled and halved shallots.

When browned, season with salt and pepper and simmer, covered, for about ten minutes.

Half way through cooking, deglaze the sauce with the *Pommeau* liqueur and add the cooked chopped bacon.

When the quails are cooked, remove from the casserole and arrange in a serving dish.

Reduce the sauce by half.

Check the seasoning and, if desired, add a few truffle shavings.

Pour the sauce over the quails and serve hot.

Cinnamon-spiced veal kidneys

Cinnamon-spiced veal kidneys

Serves 4

Preparation: 20 minutes
Cooking time: 30 minutes

2 SMALL VEAL KIDNEYS WITH FAT
6 CINNAMON STICKS
500 ML (17 FL OZ) CINNAMON-SPICED VEAL GRAVY
4 BAY LEAVES
100 ML (3.5 FL OZ) OLIVE OIL
GUÉRANDE SEA SALT
FRESHLY GROUND PEPPER

Using a knife, remove the excess fat from the kidneys so, where possible, there is an even, 1 cm layer of fat all the way round.
Stud the kidneys with the cinnamon sticks and, using a knife, make small incisions and insert the bay leaves.
Season generously with pepper and sprinkle salt over the kidney fat.
Brown the kidneys on all sides in hot olive oil and then leave to cook in their fat for 30 minutes with the lid on the pan. Turn and baste regularly.
Check to see if the kidneys are cooked by inserting a knife into the thickest part. The tip of the knife should be warm to the touch.
When cooked, leave the kidneys to rest in the pan for at least ten minutes.
Meanwhile heat the cinnamon-spiced gravy.
When the ten minutes are up, remove most of the fat from the kidneys and cut into thick slices.
Sprinkle with Guérande sea salt and serve with the gravy on the side.

Newfoundland cod *minchie*

Serves 4

Preparation: 30 minutes
Cooking time: 30 minutes

4 SALTED COD FILLETS, SOAKED
1 DOZEN NEW POTATOES
2 OR 3 ONIONS
2 OR 3 SHALLOTS
1 GARLIC CLOVE
A LITTLE PARSLEY
1 KNOB OF BUTTER
1 LARGE BOUQUET GARNI WITH THYME, BAY LEAVES AND LEEKS
FRESHLY GROUND SALT AND PEPPER

Cut the peeled potatoes into rounds and place in a cast-iron casserole.
Add the finely sliced onions and shallots and cover with water.
Add the parsley, bouquet garni and peeled garlic clove. Season and cook for 20 to 25 minutes.
When the potatoes are cooked, add the four soaked cod fillets to the casserole, season with salt and pepper and add a knob of butter to each fillet. Cover and cook for 4 to 5 minutes.
When ready, bring the casserole to the table so that your guests can help themselves.

Newfoundland cod minchie

Shoulder of salt-meadow lamb with *boulangère* potatoes

Serves 6 to 8

Preparation: 15 minutes
Cooking time: 55 minutes

1 shoulder of salt-meadow lamb from the Bay of Mont-Saint-Michel weighing 1.5 kg (3.3 lb) to 2 kg (4.4 lb)
6 onions
1.2 kg (2.7 lb) large potatoes
1 bouquet garni
1 glass of dry cider
50 g (2 oz) butter
freshly ground salt and pepper

Preheat the oven to 200°C (400°F/Gas mark 6).
Place the lamb in a buttered oven dish and cook for 20 minutes.
Meanwhile, peel and finely slice the onions and potatoes. Do not rinse the potatoes once sliced.
Fry the onions in a little butter until golden.
Take the lamb out of the oven and remove it from the dish. Add the mixed and seasoned onions and potatoes to the dish with the bouquet garni.
Pour in the cider and then cover the vegetables with water.
Put the lamb back in the dish and cook for another thirty minutes.
Cut the lamb into thin slices and serve with the *boulangère* potatoes.

Pheasant and apple casserole

Serves 4

Preparation: 30 minutes
Cooking time: 50 minutes

1 pheasant, gutted but with liver
100 g (3.5 oz) pig liver
4 apples
60 g (2 oz) butter
1 egg
1 spoonful of yoghurt
a little flat leaf parsley
1 shallot
1 garlic clove
1 pork bard
50 ml (1.7 fl oz) *Calvados*
1 glass of water
a few fresh herb leaves
freshly ground salt and pepper

Finely chop the pig liver, pheasant liver and shallot. Then mix with the yoghurt, egg, parsley and chopped garlic.
Stuff the pheasant with the mixture and then tie a layer of pork bard around it. Season with salt and pepper.
Melt the butter in a casserole and brown the pheasant, on all sides, for 5 minutes.
Cook for another ten minutes and then add the peeled and quartered apples.
Cook for a further 10 minutes.
Flambé the pheasant and apple with the *Calvados*.
Add the glass of water. Check the seasoning and finish cooking, basting regularly.
When cooked, remove the pheasant from the casserole and cut into pieces.
Arrange the pheasant in the centre of a serving dish with the stuffing on top.
Surround with the apple pieces and pour over the gravy.
Garnish with a few fresh herb leaves.

Shoulder of salt-meadow lamb with boulangère potatoes

Autumn Desserts

Honey-flavoured rice flan

Serves 4 to 6
Preparation: 8 minutes for the rice pudding, 15 minutes for the flan
Cooking time: 35 minutes for the rice pudding, 25 minutes for the flan

For the rice pudding:

125 G (4.5 OZ) ROUND GRAIN RICE
500 ML (17 FL OZ) MILK
1/2 VANILLA POD
25 G (1 OZ) BUTTER
50 G (2 OZ) CASTER SUGAR
1 PINCH OF SALT
1 LITRE (1 3/4 PINTS) WATER

For the flan:

500 ML RICE PUDDING
3 TBSP HONEY
2 EGG WHITES - 2 EGG YOLKS
4 PEARS, FINELY SLICED
6 TBSP SUGAR
50 G (2 OZ) CANDIED FRUIT
50 G (2 OZ) BUTTER
1 PINCH OF SALT

Boil the rice in 1 litre (1 3/4 pints) of water for 4 to 5 minutes.
In another pan, boil the milk and vanilla pod.
Drain the rice, remove the vanilla pod from the milk and then pour the rice into the milk. Add the butter and a pinch of salt and cook on a low heat for 15 minutes, stirring regularly.
Add the sugar, cook for another fifteen minutes and then leave to cool.
Then add the honey, egg yolks and candied fruit to the rice pudding.
Whisk the egg whites with a pinch of salt until stiff and then mix all the ingredients together.
Butter an oven-proof porcelain dish and spoon in half of the rice pudding mixture.
Add the pear slices and sprinkle with sugar.
Spoon on the remaining rice pudding and sprinkle with sugar again.
Dot with small knobs of butter and bake for 25 minutes at 180-200°C (350-400°F/Gas mark 4-6).
If necessary, brown the sugar topping under the grill and then serve, hot or cold, with a glass of perry.

Chouchen-flavoured caramel custard

Serves 4

Preparation: 20 minutes
Cooking time: 30 minutes

300 ML (1/2 PINT) *CHOUCHEN* MEAD
500 ML (17 FL OZ) SINGLE CREAM
50 G (2 OZ) ACACIA HONEY
1 PINCH OF CINNAMON
ZEST OF 1 ORANGE
6 EGGS

For the caramel:

15 SUGAR LUMPS
1 DASH OF LEMON JUICE
1 TSP WATER
1 TBSP WATER

Heat the *Chouchen* in a pan and boil for 1 to 2 minutes.
Then add the honey, cream, orange zest and pinch of cinnamon.
Beat the eggs in a separate bowl, pour in the warm *Chouchen* and mix.
To make the caramel, put the sugar lumps and lemon juice in a pan with the tablespoon of water.
Heat over a high heat until the sugar turns to caramel.
When the caramel is ready, add the teaspoon of water to prevent further cooking and then pour into a sandwich tin.
Pour the *Chouchen* mixture into the tin, place in a bain marie and cook in the oven at 180°C (350°F/Gas mark 4) for 30 minutes.
Leave to cool and turn out of the tin just before serving.

Honey-flavoured rice flan

My special Tarte Tatin recipe

Serves 4 to 6

Preparation: 15 minutes
Cooking time: 40 minutes

8 LARGE APPLES (BOSKOOP, REINE DES REINETTES, ROYAL GALA OR IDARED), PEELED
100 G (3.5 OZ) BUTTER
150 G (5 OZ) SUGAR
150 ML *CALVADOS*
400 G (14 OZ) SHORTCRUST PASTRY
200 ML (7 FL OZ) DOUBLE CREAM

Melt the butter in a non-stick pan, add the sugar and caramelise lightly.
Remove from the heat and add the apples, cut into quarters.
Return to the heat, caramelise the apples and flambé with *Calvados*.
Arrange the apples in a non-stick tin and pour over the caramel.
Roll out the pastry to form a round the size of the tin and use to cover the apples.
Oven bake at 180°C (350°F/Gas mark 4) for 30 minutes.
Remove from the oven and leave to cool slightly.
Turn out onto a serving dish.
Serve with crème fraîche on the side.

My special Tarte Tatin recipe

Pears in puff pastry parcels

Serves 4

Preparation: 20 minutes
Cooking time: 35 minutes

400 G (14 OZ) PUFF PASTRY
8 SMALL PEARS
50 G (2 OZ) BUTTER
1 TBSP CASTER SUGAR
1 EGG YOLK
1 TBSP SINGLE CREAM

Preheat the oven to 180°C (350°F/Gas mark 4).
Peel and core the pears, place a knob of butter in the hollow then roll in the caster sugar.
Bake the pears for about ten minutes, basting regularly.
When cooked, remove from the oven and leave to cool.
Keep the oven on.
Roll out the pastry to a couple of millimetres thick and cut into eight squares.
Place a pear in the centre of each square.
Bring the corners of the square together to form a parcel, pulling gently on the pastry. Then seal the edges by pinching them together.
Beat the egg and cream and use to glaze the parcels.
Bake for 25 to 30 minutes and serve warm or hot.

For this recipe, Annette used small, irregular-shaped pears that could not be sold but were nice and tasty.

Belle Annette pears

Serves 6

Preparation: 20 minutes
Cooking time: 20 minutes

6 CONFERENCE PEARS
60 G (2 OZ) CASTER SUGAR
100 G (3.5 OZ) DARK COOKING CHOCOLATE
30 G (1.1 OZ) BUTTER
1 LITRE (1 3/4 PINTS) VANILLA ICE CREAM

Peel the pears, leaving them whole with their stalks intact.
Using a sharp knife, core the pears from the bottom.
Place in a pan with the sugar, cover with water and cook for 20 minutes.
When cooked, remove from the pan and keep in the fridge.
Reduce the syrup by three-quarters and then melt the chocolate, broken into pieces, in the syrup.
Add the butter and gently stir to form a smooth sauce.
Divide the ice cream into six servings and use to stuff the bottom of each pear.
Stand the pears in bowls or dishes and top with the chocolate sauce.

Prune and golden raisin custard flan

Serves 4

Preparation: 20 minutes
Marinade: overnight
Cooking time: about 2 hours

120 G (4.2 OZ) GOLDEN RAISINS
400 G (14 OZ) PRUNES, PITTED
250 G (9 OZ) FLOUR
1 PINCH OF SALT
40 G (1.5 OZ) CASTER SUGAR
5 EGGS
200 ML (7 FL OZ) MILK
200 ML (7 FL OZ) SINGLE CREAM
20 G (0.7 OZ) SALTED BUTTER
TEA
ICING SUGAR

The night before, put the raisins in a bowl with the hot tea.
Leave to soak and then add the pitted prunes. Mix well and leave to infuse overnight.
The next day, mix the sifted flour in a bowl with the sugar and salt.
Break the eggs into another bowl and beat lightly.
Make a well in the flour and incorporate the eggs.
Mix in the milk and warm cream until the mixture is smooth.
Add the marinated raisins and prunes.
Pour the mixture into a buttered tin and cook for 1 hour at 180°C (350°F/Gas mark 4) and then 1 hour at 150°C (300°F/Gas mark 2).
Remove from the oven and dust with icing sugar.

Autumn grape terrine

Serves 4

Preparation: 20 minutes
Cooking time: 40 minutes

200 G (7 OZ) SIFTED FLOUR
300 G (10.5 OZ) GREEN AUTUMN GRAPES
4 EGGS
150 G (5 OZ) SUGAR
1 SACHET OF BAKING POWDER
2 TBSP FROMAGE BLANC
1 SPOONFUL OF BUTTER
2 TBSP SWEET WHITE WINE
ICING SUGAR
1 PINCH OF SALT

The night before, thoroughly wash the grapes, dry them in a tea towel and remove the seeds.
Leave out overnight.
The next day, separate the egg whites and yolks.
Whisk the yolks and sugar until light and fluffy.
Add the fromage blanc, white wine, sifted flour and baking powder and mix again.
In another bowl, whisk the egg whites with a pinch of salt until stiff.
Fold the whites into the mixture.
Butter and flour a terrine dish.
Pour in half the mixture, then 200 g (7 oz) of the grapes, cover with the remaining mixture and bake at 180°C (350°F/Gas mark 4) for 40 minutes.
Leave to cool.
Turn out of the dish, dust with icing sugar and surround with the remaining 100 g (3.5 oz) grapes.

Prune and raisin custard flan

Chocolate and orange mousse

Serves 4 to 6

Preparation: 30 to 40 minutes

180 G (6.3 OZ) DARK CHOCOLATE
1 TBSP FULL CREAM MILK
100 ML (3.5 FL OZ) SINGLE CREAM
20 G (0.7 OZ) BUTTER
3 EGGS
20 G (0.7 OZ) ICING SUGAR
50 G (2 OZ) CANDIED ORANGE SEGMENTS
10 G (0.35 OZ) CANDIED ORANGE PEEL
SPRIGS OF MINT

Finely chop the chocolate with a knife and put in a large bowl with the candied orange peel.
Heat the milk and cream to about 40°C and then pour over the chocolate.
Whisk in the butter, cut into small pieces.
Separate the egg whites and yolks.
Whisk the whites until stiff and then mix in the yolks.
Carefully fold the eggs into the chocolate.
Pour the mixture into a large earthenware bowl and chill.
Decorate with chocolate shavings, sprigs of wild mint and candied orange segments. Dust with icing sugar.

Chocolate and orange mousse

Baked apples

Baked apples

Wash and core the apples without peeling them.
Make an incision half way up each apple (and cut the skin all the way around).
Preheat the oven to 180°C (350°F/Gas mark 4).
Mix the cinnamon, sugar and unsalted and salted butter together and then use to fill the cored apples.
Place the apples in a buttered oven-proof dish. Add a few spoonfuls of water and bake for 1 1/4-1 1/2 hours.
Baste regularly and when the apples come out of the oven, put a teaspoon of the jelly or jam on top of each one and sprinkle with a few flaked almonds.
Serve in the dish while still hot.

Serves 4

Preparation: 15 minutes
Cooking time: 1 1/4 hours

4 APPLES (BOSKOOP, REINETTE, CANADA, ETC.)
2 TSP CINNAMON POWDER
60 G (2 OZ) CASTER SUGAR
60 TO 80 G (2-3 OZ) BUTTER (HALF UNSALTED/HALF SALTED BUTTER)
1 SPOONFUL OF REDCURRANT OR STRAWBERRY JELLY OR JAM
A FEW FLAKED ALMONDS
A FEW SPOONFULS OF WATER

Winter Recipes

The lovely eggs chosen by La Mère Poulard will end up in the frying pan as light and fluffy omelettes and the plump free-range chickens will be cooked on spits in the fire and enjoyed on winter evenings.

Winter Starters

Farmhouse bacon and bean soup

Serves 8 to 10

Preparation: 30 minutes
Cooking time: 1 hour

200 G (7 OZ) DRIED WHITE KIDNEY BEANS, SOAKED
2 POTATOES
2 CARROTS
2 TURNIPS
2 LEEKS
2 LARGE ONIONS
2 SHALLOTS
2 GARLIC CLOVES
200 G (7 OZ) THICK FARMHOUSE BACON
50 G (2 OZ) BUTTER
2 LITRES (3 1/2 PINTS) CHICKEN STOCK
1 LITRE (1 3/4 PINTS) WATER
A FEW SPRIGS OF PARSLEY
A FEW CROUTONS
FRESHLY GROUND SALT AND PEPPER

Peel, wash and dry all the vegetables.
Cut into small, irregular-shaped pieces.
Fry the vegetables in a large pan with a knob of butter.
Cut the bacon into cubes and then add to the vegetables.
Add the beans.
Cover with the chicken stock and water and simmer for about 1 hour.
Regularly skim off the foam.
Add a little salt and a generous helping of pepper.
Serve in small bowls that have been rubbed with garlic.
Add a few croutons and garnish with freshly chopped parsley.

Cream of mushroom and chestnut soup

Serves 4

Preparation: 15 minutes
Cooking time: 30 minutes

100 G (3.5 OZ) CHESTNUTS, PEELED
100 G (3.5 OZ) BUTTON MUSHROOMS
1 LITRE (1 3/4 PINTS) CHICKEN OR BEEF STOCK
200 G (7 OZ) SINGLE CREAM
JUICE OF 1 LEMON
A FEW FRESH HERB LEAVES
1 PINCH OF NUTMEG
2 SHALLOTS, FINELY CHOPPED
1 KNOB OF SALTED BUTTER
FRESHLY GROUND SALT AND PEPPER

Thoroughly wash the mushrooms and then pat dry.
Sweat the shallots in a pan with the butter and then add the whole mushrooms and chestnuts.
Add the lemon juice and grated nutmeg and then cover with the stock and cream.
Cook for about thirty minutes.
Season with salt and pepper.
Once the mushrooms are cooked, transfer to a blender or food processor and blend.
Sieve, if necessary, and serve hot, garnished with a few fresh herb leaves.

Farmhouse bacon and bean soup

Duck foie gras and apple terrine

Serves 8 to 10

Preparation: 30 minutes
Cooking time: 10 minutes

1 LARGE DUCK LIVER, WEIGHING ABOUT 500 G (1.1 LB)
2 SMALL APPLES (IDARED OR JONAGORED)
4 FRESH FIGS
1 PINCH OF *GUÉRANDE* SEA SALT
1 PINCH OF MIXED SPICE
FRESHLY GROUND PEPPER
A FEW CHERVIL LEAVES TO GARNISH
SLICES OF TOASTED FARMHOUSE BREAD

Duck *foie gras* and apple terrine

Separate the two *foie gras* lobes.
Carefully remove the main vein from each lobe and then cut into 1-2 cm (1/4-3/4") thick slices.
Season both sides with salt, pepper and mixed spice and fry the slices in a hot, non-stick pan for 1 to 2 minutes on each side.
Drain the *foie gras* slices on a small rack.
Recover half of the cooking fat and blend with the fresh figs.
Peel and core the apples. Cut into quarters and then fry in the remaining fat for a few minutes.
Arrange successive layers of *foie gras,* figs and apples in a terrine dish.
Cover with fat if necessary.
Weigh down the terrine and chill for 72 hours.
Cut the terrine into slices, arrange on a plate and sprinkle with *Guérande* sea salt.
Garnish with a few chervil leaves and serve with slices of toasted farmhouse bread.

New Year lobster salad

Serves 4

Preparation: 20 minutes
Cooking time: 15 minutes for the two lobsters

2 LOBSTERS, WEIGHING 500 TO 600 G (1.1-1.3 LB)
200 G (7 OZ) MIXED GREEN LETTUCE
300 ML (1/2 PINT) VINAIGRETTE MADE FROM
200 ML (7 FL OZ) SINGLE CREAM,
50 ML (1.7 FL OZ) OLIVE OIL,
10 G (0.35 OZ) FRESH TRUFFLES, CHOPPED,
SALT AND PEPPER AND
50 ML (1.7 FL OZ) BALSAMIC VINEGAR
ONIONS STUDDED WITH CLOVES
1 CARROT
2 LEEK GREENS
PARSLEY
FRESHLY GROUND SALT AND PEPPER

Boil the two lobsters in a court bouillon, seasoned with salt, pepper, clove-studded onions, the carrot, leek greens and parsley, for 15 minutes.
Meanwhile, thoroughly wash the mixed lettuce.
Arrange the lettuce on four plates.
Drain the cooked lobster and carefully remove the meat while still hot. Use gloves so as not to burn your hands.
Cut the meat into thick rounds.
Arrange the hot lobster meat on the lettuce and drizzle with the truffle vinaigrette.

New Year lobster salad

Serves 4

Preparation: 25 minutes
Cooking time: 5 minutes under the grill (200°C/400°F/Gas mark 6)

20 FLAT CANCALE OYSTERS
1/4 RIPE CAMEMBERT
4 GENEROUS SPOONFULS OF DOUBLE CREAM
1 LARGE HANDFUL OF FRESHLY PICKED NETTLE LEAVES
1 PINCH OF SALT AND PEPPER
20 G (0.7 OZ) BUTTER

Cancale oysters with Camembert and peppered nettles

Shuck the oysters, leaving them in their bottom shell.
Then sweat the chopped nettles in a little butter, as you would spinach.
Add the cream, Camembert (cut into small cubes) and a little salt and pepper and then reduce to form a creamy sauce.
Pour this nettle and cream sauce over the oysters.
Then pop the oysters under the grill for a few minutes until golden.
Serve immediately.

A tip to keep the oysters flat and stop them from losing their water – arrange them on a pile of cooking salt.

Cancale oysters with Camembert and peppered nettles

Chitterling sausage, apple and potato tatin

Chitterling sausage, apple and potato tatin

Serves 4

Preparation: 25 minutes
Cooking time: 30 minutes

- 1/2 chitterling sausage, weighing 500 to 600 g (1.1 lb-1.3 lb)
- 5 or 6 Charlotte potatoes
- 2 Reinette apples
- 1 large slice of smoked bacon
- 3 or 4 shallots, chopped
- A little butter
- 3 or 4 tbsp cider vinegar
- 100 g (3.5 oz) thick cream
- 1 pinch of salt and pepper
- Parsley to garnish

Remove the sausage skin and set aside. Cook the potatoes in their skins, like in the olden days, adding a little smoked bacon to give them flavour. Peel and slice the apples and then lightly fry them in a little butter.

Arrange successive layers of potato, apple and sausage in a large, greased ovenproof dish.

When the dish is full, pop in the oven for 7 to 8 minutes at 160-180°C (325-350°F/Gas mark 3-4).

Bring the dish to the table but unlike traditional tatins, do not serve it upside down. Serve with the following sauce: reduce the cider vinegar, chopped sausage skin and chopped shallots until thick like honey. Then add the cream and reduce again. Sieve the sauce, season with salt and pepper and then pour over the tatin.

Garnish with sprigs of parsley and serve with a small curly endive salad and chopped warm bacon.

Pan-fried prawns from the bay

Pan-fried prawns from the bay

Melt the butter with the thyme and bay leaves in a heavy based pan.
Add the prawns and cover.
Sauté the prawns and when cooked, season generously with salt and pepper.
Wrap them in a thick tea towel for a few minutes and then bring to the table while still warm.
Serve with salted butter and warm slices of farmhouse bread.

Serves 4

Preparation: 10 to 15 minutes
Cooking time: 3 to 6 minutes, depending on the size

600 G UNCOOKED PRAWNS
4 SPRIGS OF THYME
4 BAY LEAVES
1 PINCH OF *GUÉRANDE* SEA SALT
A FEW TWISTS OF PEPPER
50 G (2 OZ) SALTED BUTTER

Warm chicken liver salad with sauerkraut

Peel and finely chop the shallots then brown in a casserole with 10 g (0.35 oz) of butter.
Pour in the *Pommeau* liqueur, season with salt and pepper and stir.
Reduce the liquid until it resembles a thick syrup.
Add the oil and vinegar and then set to one side.
Slowly reheat the sauerkraut in a pan.
Slice the chicken liver and fry in the remaining half of butter for a few minutes, being careful not to overcook it.
Arrange the sauerkraut in the middle of the plates and then top with the chicken liver.
Drizzle with the warm vinaigrette and garnish with the finely chopped parsley, chives and shallots.

Serves 4

Preparation: 15 minutes
Cooking time: 15 minutes

400 G (14 OZ) CHICKEN LIVER
200 G (7 OZ) SAUERKRAUT, COOKED
20 G (0.7 OZ) BUTTER
2 SHALLOTS
1 GLASS OF *POMMEAU* LIQUEUR

For the vinaigrette:
OIL
VINEGAR
CHIVES
CHOPPED PARSLEY
FRESHLY GROUND SALT AND PEPPER

Winter Main Courses

La Mère Poulard's Normandy sole fillets

Serves 4

Preparation: 30 minutes
Cooking time: 10 minutes

8 SOLE FILLETS
A FEW MUSSELS FROM THE BAY, SHELLED
8 LARGE BLAINVILLE OYSTERS
8 SMALL DUBLIN BAY PRAWNS, PEELED
A FEW WINKLES, SHELLED
2 LARGE GLASSES OF DRY CIDER
5 OR 6 SPOONFULS OF THICK CREAM
1 GENEROUS SPOONFUL OF BUTTER
CHERVIL OR PARSLEY
FRESHLY GROUND SALT AND PEPPER

Put the sole, mussels, oysters, Dublin Bay prawns, winkles and butter in a pan, add salt, pepper and the cider and simmer for a few minutes.
Once cooked, strain the cooking liquid and reduce it by three quarters in another pan. Add the cream and cook for another few minutes, then check the seasoning.
Arrange the sole on warm plates with the seafood and creamy sauce.
Garnish with a few herbs and serve.

Mont-Saint-Michel tuna casserole

Serves 4

Preparation: 20 minutes
Cooking time: 45 minutes

1 THICK TUNA STEAK, WEIGHING ABOUT 800 G (1.8 LB)
500 ML (17 FL OZ) CIDER
4 ONIONS, CHOPPED
400 G (14 OZ) BUTTON MUSHROOMS, WASHED AND ROUGHLY CHOPPED
2 GARLIC CLOVES, CHOPPED AND CRUSHED
1 BOUQUET GARNI
30 G (1 OZ) FLOUR
50 G (2 OZ) DOUBLE CREAM
3 TBSP OLIVE OIL
20 G (0.7 OZ) BUTTER
SOME FRESH HERB LEAVES
FRESHLY GROUND SALT AND PEPPER

Season the tuna with salt and pepper then fry in a little olive oil for about 10 minutes.
Meanwhile, brown the onions in a pan with a little butter, then add the tuna.
Fry the mushrooms in another pan with the rest of the olive oil.
When the tuna is brown in colour remove it from the pan and add a little flour to the onions. Cook the flour a little and then add the cider, bouquet garni and garlic.
Mix well and then return the tuna to the pan and cook on a low heat for 25 to 30 minutes.
When nearly cooked, add the mushrooms and simmer for a few minutes.
Cut the tuna on your serving dish and top with the sauce.
Pour on the warm, reduced cream and garnish with some fresh herb leaves.

La Mère Poulard's Normandy sole fillets

Trout papillote-style with chicory

Trout papillote-style with chicory

Serves 4

Preparation: 10 minutes
Cooking time: 15 minutes

4 PIECES OF TROUT, WEIGHING 200 G (7 OZ) OR 1 LARGE TROUT WEIGHING 600 TO 800 G (1.3-1.8 LB)
20 TO 30 CHICORY LEAVES
2 SHALLOTS, CHOPPED
4 TBSP COURT BOUILLON
2 TSP OLIVE OIL
1 LEMON, SLICED
400 ML (13.5 FL OZ) BEURRE BLANC
FRESHLY GROUND SALT AND PEPPER

Gut, prepare and then season the trout with salt and pepper.
Wrap the trout in the blanched chicory leaves and then put them on four large sheets of tin foil.
Drizzle with the court bouillon and add the shallots, olive oil and a few lemon slices.
Wrap the trout in the tin foil and seal to make parcels, put them in an oven-proof dish and bake at 240°C (475°F/Gas mark 9) for 15 minutes.
Remove from the oven and serve in their parcels with beurre blanc.

(Note: if you choose to cook 1 large trout, you will only need 1 sheet of tin foil. Bake for 25 to 30 minutes at 240°C (475°F/Gas mark 9) and when cooked, cut it into slices and serve with beurre blanc.)

Cancale baked gurnard

Serves 4

Preparation: 15 minutes
Cooking time: 20 + 15 minutes

4 GURNARD FILLETS
2 TOMATOES
2 SHALLOTS, CHOPPED
150 G (5 OZ) BUTTON MUSHROOMS, WASHED AND CHOPPED
2 GLASSES OF DRY CIDER
1 GLASS OF WATER
30 G (1 OZ) BUTTER
1 TBSP FINELY CRUSHED MELBA TOAST
1 PINCH OF PARSLEY, FINELY CHOPPED
JUICE OF 1 LEMON
FRESHLY GROUND SALT AND PEPPER

Scale, wash and clean the fish or ask the fishmonger to do this for you.
Skin and deseed the tomatoes and then cut into small pieces.
Fry the shallots in the butter, add the tomatoes and mushrooms and cook for 5 minutes.
Then add the parsley and crushed melba toast and cover with the cider and water. Add salt and pepper, mix well and simmer for 10 to 15 minutes, stirring often.
Pour some of the mixture into a greased oven-proof dish, add the fish and then cover with the rest of the mixture.
Bake at 220°C (450°F/Gas mark 8) for 15 minutes.
Remove from the oven, drizzle with lemon juice and serve.

Black pudding with apples and potatoes

Serves 4

Preparation: 30 minutes for the mashed potatoes,
20 minutes for the black pudding and apples
Cooking time: 15 minutes for the black pudding and apples

200 g (7 oz) large potatoes
200 g (7 oz) apples, peeled and sliced
juice of 1 lemon
80 g (3 oz) butter
4 portions of black pudding, weighing 150 to 180 g (5-6.3 oz), salted, peppered and pricked with a fork
freshly ground salt and pepper

Cook the potatoes in lightly salted water.
When cooked, peel and mash the potatoes with 20 g (0.7 oz) of butter and keep warm.
Then mix the sliced apples with lemon juice and fry in 40 g (1.5 oz) of butter for 15 minutes, stirring occasionally.
Melt the rest of the butter in another pan and cook the black pudding for 12 to 15 minutes, turning often.
Season with salt and pepper and then arrange the apples, mashed potatoes and black pudding on a serving dish.

Black pudding with apples and potatoes

Veal parcels with prunes

Veal parcels with prunes

Serves 4

Preparation: 20 minutes
Cooking time: 45 minutes

4 THIN VEAL ESCALOPES
200 G (7 OZ) PRUNES, STONED
200 G (7 OZ) FINE STUFFING, FROM THE BUTCHER
50 G (2 OZ) BUTTER
2 SHALLOTS, CHOPPED
CIDER
1 CLOVE
300 G (10.5 OZ) FRESH PASTA
FRESHLY GROUND SALT AND PEPPER

Chop 150 g (5 oz) of the prunes and mix with the fine stuffing.
Make four balls with this mixture and place in the centre of each veal escalope.
Roll up each escalope tightly, tie with string and season with salt and pepper.
Melt the butter in a casserole and brown the veal on all sides, then add the shallots, the remaining prunes, cider and the clove.
Cover and cook on a low heat for about 45 minutes.
Halfway through cooking, check the gravy and add 2 or 3 spoonfuls of water if it is too thick.
Serve with fresh pasta.

Serves 4 to 8

Preparation: 30 minutes
Cooking time: 40 minutes

1 FARMHOUSE CHICKEN, WEIGHING 2 KG (4.4 LB)
5 OR 6 APPLES, PEELED AND QUARTERED
250 ML (9 FL OZ) CRÈME FRAÎCHE
1 GLASS OF *CALVADOS*
2 GLASSES OF DRY CIDER
4 SHALLOTS, PEELED
1 KNOB OF BUTTER
1 BUNCH OF PARSLEY
100 G (3.5 OZ) SMALL ONIONS, PEELED
A PINCH OF SALT AND PEPPER

Farmhouse chicken with cider and *Calvados*

Cut – or get your butcher to cut – the chicken into 8 pieces.
Brown the chicken in a casserole with the shallots and small onions, then flambé with the *Calvados* and add the dry cider.
Add the apples, cover and cook for about 1 hour.
When cooked, remove the chicken and continue to cook the rest for about 10 minutes.
When the sauce has thickened, add the crème fraîche and reduce for 10 to 15 minutes until creamy.
Reheat the chicken in a small casserole and then pour on the sauce.
Add a small knob of butter to the gravy, garnish with parsley and add a pinch of freshly ground pepper if necessary.
Serve hot with a few roasted quarters of apple around the chicken.

Farmhouse chicken with cider and Calvados

Spit-roasted Bayeux pork with honey and Chouchen mead

Spit-roasted Bayeux pork with honey and *Chouchen* mead

Insert sprigs of rosemary into the pork, rub the meat with coarse sea salt and marinate in honey and *Chouchen* mead overnight.

The next day, roast the pork on a spit over a low heat for 1 1/2 to 2 hours, collecting the fat in a dripping pan.

When cooked, leave to rest, then cut into slices and drizzle with the fat. Sprinkle on some sea salt and a pinch of pepper.

Serve hot with potatoes baked in the embers in the skins.

Serves 4 to 6

Preparation: 15 to 20 minutes
Cooking time: 1 1/2 to 2 hours, depending on the size.

1 LOIN OF BAYEUX PORK,
4 TO 6 RIBS
50 G (2 OZ) HONEY
300 ML (1/2 PINT) *CHOUCHEN* MEAD
COARSE SEA SALT
1 SPOONFUL OF SEA SALT
FRESHLY GROUND PEPPER
2 SPRIGS OF ROSEMARY
600 G (1.3 LB) POTATOES, RATTE OR CHARLOTTE

Winter Desserts

Lemon cake

Serves 6 to 8

Preparation: 20 minutes
Cooking time: 40 minutes

3 LARGE EGGS
170 G (6 OZ) CASTER SUGAR
170 G (6 OZ) FLOUR, SIFTED
170 G (6 OZ) BUTTER
1 PINCH OF SALT
40 ML (1.5 FL OZ) *CALVADOS*
JUICE OF 2 LEMONS
ZESTS OF THE 2 LEMONS, CANDIED

Melt the butter and sift the flour.
Separate the egg whites and yolks and then whisk the whites with a little salt until stiff.
Preheat the oven to 210°C (425°F/Gas mark 7).
Beat the egg yolks and sugar until light and fluffy. Add the melted butter, flour, *Calvados,* zests and lemon juice.
Then carefully fold in the egg whites.
Grease and flour a 20 to 25 cm (8-10") cake tin, pour in the mixture and bake for 10 minutes.
Once the 10 minutes are up, lower the oven temperature to 160-180°C (325-350°F/Gas mark 3-4) and continue baking for 25 to 30 minutes.
Turn the cake out of the tin while it is still warm.
It can be stored for several days in a moist cloth or air-tight container.

Citrus and brown sugar gratin

Serves 4

Preparation: 10 minutes
Cooking time: 20 minutes

4 ORANGES
4 CLEMENTINES
2 GRAPEFRUIT
1 SACHET VANILLA SUGAR
1 PINCH OF CINNAMON
250 ML (9 FL OZ) MILK
2 LARGE EGGS
50 G (2 OZ) LIGHT BROWN SUGAR

Peel the fruit and separate into segments.
Preheat the oven to 180°C (350°F/Gas mark 4).
Arrange the fruit alternating the different colours in an oven-proof dish and dust with the vanilla sugar and cinnamon.
Beat the eggs, add boiling milk and brown sugar and then whisk vigorously.
Pour this mixture over the fruit and bake for about 20 minutes.
Remove from the oven and leave to cool before serving.

Lemon cake

Apple meringue pie

Serves 4

Preparation: 20 minutes
Cooking time: 1 hour

500 G (1.1 LB) SHORTCRUST PASTRY
1 KG (2.2 LB) APPLES, PEELED AND QUARTERED
125 G (4.5 OZ) BUTTER
60 G (2 OZ) CASTER SUGAR
1 SACHET OF VANILLA SUGAR
100 G (3.5 OZ) APRICOT JAM
1 EGG WHITE
150 G (5 OZ) ICING SUGAR
A FEW DROPS OF LEMON JUICE

Fry the apples in the butter, add the vanilla sugar, caster sugar and apricot jam and then leave to stew for about 10 minutes.
Line a flan tin with the shortcrust pastry and once the apple mixture has cooled, pour it into the pastry case.
Mix the egg white, icing sugar and drops of lemon juice together and then whisk vigorously. Spread this mixture over the apples (it should look more like royal icing than meringue).
Bake at 160°C (325°F/Gas mark 3) for 1 hour.
If the pie cooks too quickly, lower the oven temperature.

Apple meringue pie

Sugared almond millefeuille

Sugared almond millefeuille

Serves 4

Preparation: 40 minutes
Cooking time: 20 minutes

500 G (1.1 LB) PUFF PASTRY, ROLLED AND FOLDED 6 TIMES
2 TBSP CHOPPED HAZELNUT, ALMOND AND PISTACHIO MIX
50 G (2 OZ) ICING SUGAR
300 ML (1/2 PINT) WHIPPED CREAM
300 G (10.5 OZ) CONFECTIONER'S CUSTARD
50 G (2 OZ) PRALINE, HAZELNUTS, ALMONDS

Cut the pastry into three 20 cm x 8 cm (8"/3") strips and sprinkle with the hazelnut, almond and pistachio mix.
Bake for 20 minutes.
Once 10 minutes are up, level the rising pastry by resting a shelf on a few round rings, 4 cm (1.5") above it. Dust the pastry with icing sugar and continue baking for the remaining 10 minutes.
Check whether the pastry is cooked by lightly pressing on it. You should hear a slight crackling sound.
Remove from the oven and leave to cool for 1 hour.
Meanwhile, prepare the custard and add the praline, hazelnuts and pistachios.
When the custard is cold, add the whipped cream and mix carefully.
Build the millefeuille, alternating layers of pastry and custard and then use a serrated knife to carefully cut the millefeuille into slices.

Calvados soufflé

Calvados soufflé

Warm the confectioner's custard in a pan and add the *Calvados,* stewed apple and egg yolks.
Whisk the egg whites until stiff and carefully add the confectioner's custard.
Grease and sugar the soufflé tins, pour in the mixture and bake at 180-200°C (350-400°F/Gas mark 4-6) for 15 to 20 minutes.
Remove from the oven and dust with a little icing sugar.

Serves 4

Preparation: 20 to 30 minutes
Cooking time: 15 to 20 minutes

1 BOWL OF CONFECTIONER'S CUSTARD, WITH 15 G (0.5 OZ) TAPIOCA
2 EGG YOLKS
8 EGG WHITES
2 SPOONFULS OF *CALVADOS*
1 SPOONFULS OF STEWED APPLE
1 TBSP BUTTER
50 G (2 OZ) SUGAR
SOME ICING SUGAR TO DECORATE

Chestnut and coffee mousse

Mix the butter, coffee essence, water and chestnut purée together in a large mixing bowl.
Then, make some meringue in a bain marie in the oven using the egg white.
Cook until the white is firm and shiny and then dust with icing sugar.
Combine the two mixtures and serve cold, decorated with a few slivers of candied chestnuts or drops of coffee liqueur.

Serves 4

Preparation: a few minutes

200 G (7 OZ) CHESTNUT PURÉE
100 G (3.5 OZ) BUTTER
1 TSP COFFEE ESSENCE
70 G (2.5 OZ) ICING SUGAR
2 TBSP WATER
1 EGG WHITE
A FEW SLIVERS OF CANDIED CHESTNUTS OR A FEW DROPS OF COFFEE LIQUEUR

Crunchy apple and cider custard tart

Peel the apples and cut into quarters.
Melt the butter and then add the sugar and apples to caramelise.
Then sift the flour into a mixing bowl, make a well in the centre and add a pinch of salt.
Beat the eggs and add to the flour. Mix well and then incorporate the milk and cider.
Knead the pastry until smooth and then add a spoonful of vanilla essence.
Preheat the oven to 200°C (400°F/Gas mark 6).
Grease and flour a flan tin and line it with the pastry. Add the caramelised apples and bake for 45 minutes.
Remove the flan from the oven and leave it to cool down completely before turning it out of the tin.

Serves 4

Preparation: 20 minutes
Cooking time: 45 minutes

For the cider tart:
200 G (7 OZ) FLOUR
100 G (3.5 OZ) CASTER SUGAR
4 EGGS
500 ML (17 FL OZ) MILK
500 ML (17 FL OZ) SWEET CIDER
30 G (1 OZ) BUTTER
SOME VANILLA ESSENCE
A PINCH OF SALT

For the crunchy apples:
4 APPLES
100 G (3.5 OZ) BUTTER
100 G (3.5 OZ) SUGAR

Preparation: 10 to 15 minutes
Cooking time: depending on the oven, cooking time may vary between 6 and 8 hours.

1.5 LITRES (2 1/2 PINTS) UNPASTEURISED MILK
120 G (4.2 OZ) ROUND GRAIN RICE
150 G (5 OZ) SUGAR
1 PINCH OF SALT
1 VANILLA POD
2 TSP CINNAMON
1 BAY LEAF

Normandy *teurgoule* rice pudding

Put the rice, bay leaf, split vanilla pod, sugar, salt and cinnamon in a terrine dish and cover with the cold milk.
Bake at 100°C (200°F/Gas mark 1/4) for 6 to 8 hours.

(Note: In some Normandy villages, people still take their *teurgoules* to the local bakery for cooking.)

Makes 30 profiteroles

Preparation: 45 minutes
Cooking time: 15 minutes

For the chocolate sauce:
200 G (7 OZ) QUALITY CHOCOLATE
100 ML (3.5 FL OZ) SINGLE CREAM

For the whipped cream:
400 G (14 OZ) SINGLE CREAM
75 G (3 OZ) CASTER SUGAR
1 SACHET OF VANILLA SUGAR

For the choux pastry:
80 ML (3 FL OZ) WATER
100 ML (3.5 FL OZ) SINGLE CREAM
1 PINCH OF FINE SALT
1 PINCH OF CASTER SUGAR
75 G (3 OZ) BUTTER
100 G (3.5 OZ) FLOUR, SIFTED
3 OR 4 EGGS
1 EGG FOR GLAZING

Chocolate profiteroles

Prepare the choux pastry as follows: pour the water and cream into a pan and add the salt, sugar and butter. Stir and bring to the boil. Add all the flour in one go and stir vigorously until the mixture is no longer sticky. Continue stirring to cool the mixture slightly.
Transfer to a mixing bowl and gradually beat in the eggs one by one.
Beat well to get plenty of air into the mixture and then wrap in cling film.
Preheat the oven to 200°C (400°F/Gas mark 6).
Put the mixture in a piping bag and pipe 30 small balls onto a baking sheet lined with greaseproof paper.
Beat an egg and use to glaze each ball.
Bake for 15 minutes, opening the oven door after 5 minutes.
Meanwhile, make the chocolate sauce by boiling the cream and adding the chocolate, broken into pieces.
When the chocolate has melted, stir it gently and put in a bain marie in the oven to keep warm.
Whip the cream in a chilled mixing bowl and gradually add the caster and vanilla sugar.
When the profiteroles have cooled down, open them up and insert the whipped cream.
Arrange in bowls, pour over the hot chocolate sauce and serve.

Normandy teurgoule rice pudding

La Mère Poulard Inn

La Mère Poulard Inn or *Auberge de la Mère Poulard* was opened in 1888 in the heart of Mont-Saint-Michel's mediaeval village.

This haven of peace is open all year round and visitors to the Wonder of the Western World can relax here and enjoy wonderful cuisine.

Hotel

The cosy rooms in the *Hostellerie de la Mère Poulard* combine all the charm of days gone by with modern-day comforts.

They nestle at the foot of Mont-Saint-Michel and have wonderful views of the bay, abbey, village and gardens.

Panoramic bar

It was here that La Mère Poulard liked to spend evenings with her guests, looking out onto the bay.

This relaxing, friendly bar serves mouthwatering cocktails and quality *Calvados.*

Mère Poulard Inn, behind the ramparts.

Restaurant

La Mère Poulard Restaurant stands next to the *Salle de l'omelette,* where omelettes are still made over log fires, just like in the olden days.

La Mère Poulard's family recipes are both traditional and inventive and draw on seasonal produce. In addition to her famous omelette, visitors can enjoy Normandy *foie gras,* Mont-Saint-Michel salt-meadow lamb, Breton lobster, fish from the bay, free-range chicken, polder-grown vegetables and traditional Mère Poulard desserts.

Cookery school

In addition to your tour of the abbey and stroll along the bay, why not make time for the Mont-Saint-Michel cookery school and learn more about La Mère Poulard's famous recipes.

Reception – information
La Mère Poulard – Grande Rue
50116 LE MONT-SAINT-MICHEL France
Tel. + 33 (0)2 33 89 68 68
Fax + 33 (0)2 33 89 68 69
Website: www.mere-poulard.com
Email: hotel.mere.poulard@wanadoo.fr

Recipe Index

Winter Recipes 96

Editor: Henri Bancaud
Editorial coordination: Isabelle Rousseau
Layout: Marcel Oger,
Studio des Éditions Ouest-France
Photoengraving: Micro Lynx Renn es (35)
Printing: Mame Imprimeur in Tours (37)

Édilarge SA, Rennes
ISBN 2.7373.4042.X
Editor no.: 5230.02.03.10.06
Legal deposit: April 2006
Printed in France